D0538534

SEWING FOR ALL SEASONS

SEWING FOR ALL SEASONS

24 Stylish Projects to Stitch Throughout the Year

SUSAN BEAL

CHRONICLE BOOKS

SAN FRANCISCO

Text copyright © 2013 by Susan Beal.
Photographs copyright © 2013 by Jennifer Causey.
Illustrations copyright © 2013 by Alexis Hartman.

Library of Congress Cataloging-in-Publication Data:
Beal, Susan.
  Sewing for all seasons : 24 stylish projects to stitch throughout the year / Susan Beal.
     pages cm
  Includes index.
   ISBN 978-1-4521-1428-6   *52516647*   *11/13*
1. Sewing. 2. Clothing and dress. 3. House furnishings. I. Title.

TT705.B32 2013
646.4--dc23

            2012044544

Manufactured in China

Designed by Jody Churchfield
Styling by Rachel Plotkin

10 9 8 7 6 5 4 3 2 1

Chronicle Books LLC
680 Second Street
San Francisco, California 94107
www.chroniclebooks.com

This book is for my November baby, Everett.

CONTENTS

SPRING

SUMMER

AUTUMN

WINTER

INTRODUCTION

I worked on the idea for *Sewing for All Seasons* in the autumn, designed the first few projects for the proposal in the winter, swatched, shopped for fabrics, and sewed all spring, and finished writing everything in the summer—just in time for a celebratory barbecue with friends! The yearlong process of creating this book really made me appreciate how the changing seasons can inspire our creativity.

In my family, we are lucky to have one birthday in every season. So every few months, I try to make something fun and seasonal for a birthday present or party. My daughter, Pearl, is perfectly suited to her spring birthday: She loves bright colors and flowers, and she is always excited to have her party outside in the backyard (we do live in rainy Portland, so there's always a plan B to decorate the downstairs rec room if need be!). My husband, Andrew, is lucky to have a summer birthday, perfect for his favorite things— hiking on Mount Hood or taking a day trip to the coast—and having a laid-back picnic in the backyard with the kids.

My sweet little Everett was an autumn baby who came home from the hospital wrapped up in warm layers and still loves cuddling close. One of my favorite things I've ever made was a simple wool patchwork throw I sewed the week before he was born—cozy and comforting for holding my new little boy. And I have a winter birthday, a couple of weeks after the rush of the holidays…right when I want to have friends over for a dinner party or cocktails, and figure out what I most hope the new year will bring.

The projects in this book use simple sewing and patchwork techniques to make pretty things you'll use—or give—all year round. Patterns for many of them are right in the back of the book. The color palette in the projects deepens over the seasons, from light, bright yellows and pinks to strong, gorgeous golds and reds. Dip into your brightest fabrics for a pair of summery porch pillows, or use up lots of scraps for a modern holiday garland in icy colors, along with a matching cozy for bringing a jar of homemade hot cocoa mix or a bottle of wine to a party. Every project is easy to make your own, depending on your fabric choices and embellishments. You can switch up the seasons and make a spring Cute-as-a-Button Handbag or a fall set of Nesting Canisters. It's totally up to you.

There is also a bit of custom sizing involved. Depending on the size of your sketchbook for the Sketchbook Cover project or your tea towel for the New Year's Calendar, you'll measure and cut your fabrics and stitch your project to match your needs. And you'll design your custom-fitted Spring Flowers Wrap Skirt, Gardening Apron, or Cozy Wool Slippers based on your own measurements. After some quick and simple measurements jotted down in our handy tables, and a little math to seal the deal, you'll be sewing pretty things that fit you (or your sketchbook or your calendar) perfectly!

Happy sewing!

susan

P.S. Please visit my book website at sewingforallseasons.com for lots of project extras, photos, and sewing ideas!

MATERIALS & TOOLS

You'll need only basic sewing tools and materials to make the projects in this book. Here are some recommendations for my favorites.

MATERIALS

Binding tape: I love to make my own, but you can find packaged 1-in/2.5-cm binding tape at the fabric and crafts store in lots of great colors, often labeled "extra-wide double-fold."

Buttons: Most of the projects in this book use sew-through buttons, the kind with two or four holes to stitch through (hence the name). Shank buttons, which have an opaque, often decorative front and a channel or loop behind for sewing, are available, too. You can find beautiful new or vintage buttons for your sewing projects.

Digital camera: Snapping a photo of a patchwork in progress, or just a couple of potential fabrics together, can give a new perspective on color harmony and interest. The camera picks up things you might not have noticed, so looking at a snapshot on screen can be a useful tool for finalizing your placement or choices before sewing.

Double-sided fusible web and interfacing: I used lightweight double-sided fusible web (like Steam-A-Seam 2) to join two cotton fabrics back-to-back for my simple garlands. For sturdier projects like the Patchwork Coasters and Placemats (page 67), I use superthick heavyweight double-sided interfacing. Two brands I like are Peltex 72F and fast2fuse, both sold by the yard/meter at fabric stores. For the projects in this book, I used 44-in-/112-cm-wide interfacing, as noted in the materials lists. However, sometimes these products are available in different widths, so you may need to recalculate dimensions a bit to figure out how much you need for a particular project. Follow the manufacturer's instructions to fuse the interfacing to your fabrics.

Elastic: Flat elastic comes in many widths and styles. I used a pretty pink one with a decorative edge for my Vintage Scarf Headband (page 31), and simple white ones in different widths for my French Press Cozy (page 95) and my Sewing Organizer (page 53). You can find it in packages or by the yard/meter.

Fabric: Fabric is such a wonderful and personal element for a sewing project. I've given guidelines for what I used to sew each of the projects, but you have freedom and flexibility with the fabrics you choose. In some cases, I slightly increased the fabric yardage called for to give you some leeway on your measurements. It's always better to have too much than too little!

NOTE:

Be sure to prewash your fabric before cutting and sewing any garment project.

Home dec (decorator) weight fabric: These sturdier fabrics, like canvas, denim, or brocade, are often wider on the bolt (54 in/137 cm and even 60 in/152 cm), so a ½-yd/0.5-m piece goes a long way. They make especially nice bags, and they press and stitch very well, even on a home sewing machine.

Muslin: This basic fabric is perfect for foundation string piecing when quilting. For a single one-block potholder or a generous sixty-four-block picnic quilt, muslin adds a soft layer of stability inside your patchwork. It's inexpensive and useful for testing new patterns, too.

Quilting cotton: Usually 44 in/112 cm wide (give or take) off the bolt, quilting cottons come in gorgeous modern solids and a wonderful array of prints and patterns. Quilting cottons are perfect for many of the projects in this book and are especially nice for piecing patchwork designs, lining, and making binding tape. They also fuse well to interfacing and batting.

Wool: There are many weights of wool fabric, but some of the most useful are merino (soft and cozy for my silk-lined Cozy Wool Scarf on page 85), shirt-weight and melton (both used in the Patchwork Throw, along with merino, on page 99), and flannel (for the Cozy Wool Slippers on page 125). Wool fabrics are also frequently wider on the bolt (many I used for the projects measured 60 in/152 cm). To make the Patchwork Throw, I mixed various weights and styles of wool fabrics, and for the Cozy Wool Slippers, contributing designer Michelle Freedman felted her wool yardage in the washing machine before cutting and stitching it.

Fusible batting: This easy-to-apply batting is perfect for craft projects. I love how it adds softness, thickness, and texture to a fabric, or patchwork piece, of any weight. As with interfacing, follow the manufacturer's instructions to fuse it to your project. You can find it by the yard/meter as well. (If you can't find or don't have fusible batting on hand, you can often use regular batting and simply stitch it to the wrong side of your fabric, around the perimeter, when the instructions call for fusing it with your iron.) For quilts, like the Picnic Quilt (page 77), I recommend regular quilt batting instead of fusible.

Fusible interfacing: I use single-sided heavyweight fusible interfacing to add stability and crispness to fabrics in several of the projects in the book. Follow the manufacturer's instructions to fuse it to your fabrics.

Ribbons, laces, trims: Use new or vintage embellishments like these to add sparkle to any project. I especially like using rickrack for simple, pretty details on the Holiday Ornaments (page 107) and the Holiday Garland loops (page 105).

Snaps: I like to use large snaps for sturdiness in projects, like the Cute-as-a-Button Handbag (page 121). The snap I used in that item is a U.S. size 10 (¾ in/18 mm).

Twill tape: This neatly edged woven tape lies perfectly flat. It folds crisply and beautifully to enclose the edge of the Spring Flowers Wrap Skirt (page 41), saving you a nice chunk of time by instantly creating a waistband and hem. Twill tape is available in lots of good colors by the yard/meter, and in several widths. It has many uses: I used 2-in/5-cm tape for the skirt, and ½-in/12-mm tape for the Sketchbook Cover bookmarks (page 91) and Sewing Organizer tabs (page 53).

Velcro/hook and loop tape: This product is wonderful for a quick and simple seal, from securing a small area like the back of the Coffee Cup Cozy (page 95) to closing the bottom seam of the Porch Swing Pillows (page 61). Be sure to buy the sew-in type rather than the adhesive stick-on type. You only have to try to sew through the gummy, sticky, messy Velcro once, and ruin a needle and your fabric, to learn that lesson.

Webbing: Thick, sturdy woven cotton webbing is also available by the yard/meter and is perfect for tote bag handles.

TOOLS

Binding tape maker: I consider the binding tape maker a sewing superpower. Creating your own neatly folded binding tape out of fabric that perfectly matches (or beautifully contrasts with) your project is really fun! All the projects in this book that require binding use 1-in/2.5-cm binding tape made from 2-in/5-cm strips of fabric, which when double-folded measures ½ in/12 mm wide. A 1-in/2.5-cm binding tape maker is a great little investment.

Fabric marker: I like the water-soluble kind that creates a bright blue line (you can get other colors, too). Tailor's chalk works well on wool or dark fabrics.

Glue/hot glue gun: I like to use craft glue for attaching small embellishments and hot glue for more sturdy joins. I use hot glue for the buttons on the Café Curtain clips (page 33) and, believe it or not, for neatly closing the small turning openings on the Holiday Ornaments (page 107)!

Hand-sewing needles: A pack of sharps or other general needles will come in very handy for these projects.

Iron: A steam iron that heats up quickly is crucial for happy sewing. I also keep a small spray bottle of water on hand for pressing wool or stubbornly wrinkled cottons, and a pressing cloth for other delicate fabrics.

Pattern paper: I adore dotted or gridded semi-opaque pattern paper, sold by the yard/meter at many fabric stores. Each dot marks 1 in/2.5 cm, so it's perfect for drafting your own patterns or tracing the ones in this book. It's also durable and stands up to many, many pinnings, foldings, and markings!

Pins: I love long pins with bright, oversize orbs on the blunt ends, which are easy to see. They are often labeled "ball-point" or "quilter's" pins.

Quilt rulers and templates: Quilt rulers are best for measuring flat fabrics and for cutting along a straight, perfect edge. I keep a few sizes at my cutting table—the 24-by-5-in/61-by-12-cm size is nice for cutting fabric from selvage to selvage, and I love my 6-by-12-in/15-by-30.5-cm size for cutting or trimming smaller pieces. If you're making a whole string quilt like the Picnic Quilt (page 77), I recommend investing in a square template ruler the size of your quilt block.

Seam ripper: A seam ripper is great for quickly correcting a poorly sewn seam, or for neatly coaxing a strip of fabric into your binding tape maker.

Sewing machine: A good, reliable sewing machine is wonderful to have. Basic straight and zigzag stitches are all you'll need for these projects. But I do recommend getting a ¼-in/6-mm presser foot for patchwork projects and topstitching; these are very handy, since using the side of your presser foot as a guide keeps your stitching straight and even.

Sewing machine needles: I like to have universal, quilting, and Microtex (sharp) needles on hand, in sizes 80/12 or 90/14.

Tape measure: This flexible tool is essential for measuring everything from tiny seam allowances to the entire width of a project. Most tape measures are marked with both inches and centimeters.

Thread: Cotton and polyester sewing threads come in a rainbow of colors. Wind extra bobbins of the colors you use the most. Prewound bobbins (the store-bought ones are usually in white or off-white) are great to have on hand, too!

Rotary cutter and cutting mat: This tool is perfect for precision cutting with a quilt ruler or cutting very carefully along the edge of a marked line or paper pattern. Only use a rotary cutter on a cutting mat, and be very careful to leave it locked when you set it down—the blade is very sharp and can accidentally cut your fabric (or you!) in the blink of an eye.

Scissors: I have a sharp pair of large fabric shears on my sewing table, plus a tiny pair of scissors on a ribbon around my neck. You will also want a separate pair of paper scissors, which you use just for paper (like cutting out patterns), since paper dulls scissors quickly. Pinking shears are also very useful.

TECHNIQUES

Here are the techniques you'll use to create and sew the projects in this book. They're arranged more or less in order from where you'd start (like tracing patterns and cutting) to finishing touches like binding, and they include lots of helpful illustrations for you to reference if you get stuck. See the glossary for more details on craft techniques.

USING PATTERNS

Pattern tracing

I highly recommend using semi-opaque dotted or gridded pattern paper (see page 12) to trace patterns. For the projects in this book, first check to see if the pattern needs to be enlarged. If so, use a copier, following the machine instructions. Then, to trace a pattern, simply place a piece of dotted pattern paper over the page or enlarged version and copy it with a pencil or ballpoint pen (markers or Sharpies are likely to bleed through and mark the page). Transfer any markings like openings or loop placement on the pattern to your paper as you go. Cut the pattern out and check it

against the original. This type of pattern paper is resilient and will hold up to multiple pinnings and foldings, unlike fragile tissue-weight or newsprint papers.

Be sure to label each homemade pattern with the project name, and copy any markings on the original, such as "cut 2," or openings.

Several patterns in the book are larger than the page size, so you'll need to enlarge them using a copier. For the Spring Flowers Wrap Skirt panel pattern (page 43), I've included instructions on how to draft it directly onto your pattern paper.

Cutting without a pattern

If the project cutting dimensions are simple, of course you can just mark your fabric directly and cut it out, skipping the paper pattern step.

Cutting with a pattern

Always press your fabric before cutting. Refer to the pattern to see if you need to cut a single piece of fabric or more. If you need to cut two pieces total, an easy way to cut both at once is to fold your fabric and place the pattern over both layers. If you need multiples, I suggest cutting a maximum of four layers at a time in quilting cotton, and two at a time for the thicker home dec weights. Pin the pattern in place on the fabric and cut it out with sharp fabric scissors, or carefully cut with a rotary cutter over a cutting mat.

NOTE:

Using semi-opaque pattern paper instead of a solid opaque paper means that you can see any pattern on the fabric and "fussy-cut" to capture and place the designs you like most.

SEWING

Fabric preparation

Prewashing: Always prewash your fabrics for any garment or other fitted project to avoid later shrinkage. For patchwork and other nongarment sewing, you can choose to prewash modern quilting cottons, or just sew with them off the bolt—it's up to you. I generally prewash any vintage fabrics to ensure the colors are set, and of course to make sure they're clean. Care for wool, silk, and other specialty fabrics as the manufacturer recommends.

Pressing: Pressing your fabric well is an essential step in any sewing project. You'll use an iron (be sure it's on the right fabric setting) to press your fabric, moving it forward in a series of gliding motions to not only make your fabric lie nicely flat, but also set any seams neatly. You can protect your fabric surface from the iron with a semi-transparent muslin pressing cloth, and use a spray bottle of water on any stubborn wrinkles (this is also a wonderful technique for pressing wool).

Hand-basting

Hand-basting is a simple, quick way to join two (or more) layers of fabric securely before sewing. This technique is especially useful when working with two very different fabrics (like wool and silk in the Cozy Wool Scarf, page 85) or when you're binding around corners on a quilt or patchwork project.

To hand-baste, thread a needle with a bright or contrasting thread color and use a running stitch (simply sewing a forward line in medium or long stitches) through all layers (see fig. 1). Don't bother to knot your thread; instead, make one backstitch (simply bring your needle and thread behind where you started sewing, and make one stitch backward to secure it) at the beginning of your hand-basting, or every five or six running stitches, so you don't snag or distort your layered fabrics. For hand-basting a binding corner, just stitch through all layers of the binding tape and patchwork or quilt layers to hold them all neatly in place (see fig. 20, page 23).

fig. 1

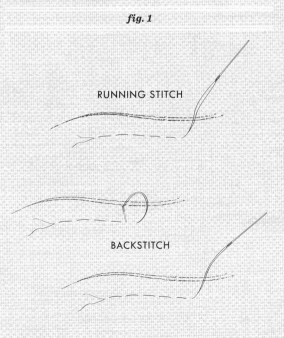

RUNNING STITCH

BACKSTITCH

Once you've finished your final sewing or binding, simply use a seam ripper or scissors to quickly remove the hand-basting threads. This is where a bright contrasting-color thread choice comes in handy!

Seams

Joining two (or more) layers of fabric together with a consistent seam allowance is a simple way to build a quality sewing project. Just line up your fabric edges exactly, pin or hold them in place, and stitch them together at a consistent width from the edge—often ¼ in/6 mm for patchwork or small projects, ½ in/12 mm for larger ones, and ⅝ in/16 mm for garments—using the markings on your sewing machine throat plate as your guide. In fig. 2, you see two examples of 3-in/7.5-cm square pieces of fabric, joined with simple seams. The ¼-in/6-mm seam is noticeably narrower than the ½-in/12-mm seam.

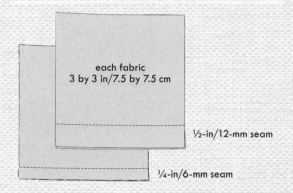

fig. 2

each fabric
3 by 3 in/7.5 by 7.5 cm

½-in/12-mm seam

¼-in/6-mm seam

After sewing, carefully press your fabric and new seams with an iron for a crisp finish. (For most of the projects in this book, I recommend pressing seams to one side rather than open for a stronger seam.) Once your fabrics are sewn, keep in mind that you will lose the total amount of the seam allowance from its length (see fig. 3). So two 3-in/7.5-cm square fabric pieces sewn together on one side with a ¼-in/6-mm seam allowance will measure 5½ by 3 in/14 by 7.5 cm

(¼ in/6 mm + ¼ in/6 mm = ½ in/12 mm in the seam), while the same square fabric pieces sewn together with a ½-in/12-mm seam allowance will measure 5 by 3 in/12 by 7.5 cm (½ in/12 mm + ½ in/12 mm = 1 in/ 2.5 cm in the seam).

Always pay attention to the seam allowance called for in the project so your finished piece is the right size, because as you can see, the difference in the measurements really adds up!

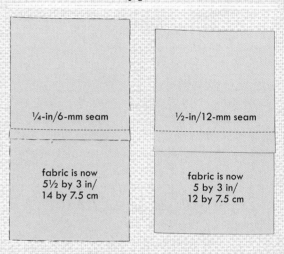

fig. 3

¼-in/6-mm seam

½-in/12-mm seam

fabric is now
5½ by 3 in/
14 by 7.5 cm

fabric is now
5 by 3 in/
12 by 7.5 cm

Backstitching

When you sew a seam or another join that's important to the stability of a project, you'll backstitch at the beginning and end of your sewing to hold the stitched seam securely. Simply start by sewing forward using the correct seam allowance, and then press the reverse button on your machine to backstitch over those first stitches, reinforcing them. Then stitch forward again and complete the seam. You'll backstitch the same way to end the seam, too.

Topstitching

Topstitching is a basic machine-sewing technique that adds stability to seams, joins fabric layers, or simply adds a polished look. To topstitch, first press your fabric, including pressing any seam allowances to one side. Working on the right side of the fabric, and catching all layers of your pressed seam underneath, stitch parallel to the seam line at a width called for in the instructions, or at the width you like. This technique creates a neat, consistent line that parallels the seam you are following. I usually topstitch about ⅛ in/3 mm away from my seams, but the width is up to you; just be consistent.

fig. 5

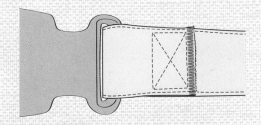

fig. 4

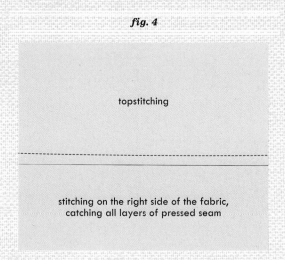

topstitching

stitching on the right side of the fabric,
catching all layers of pressed seam

Edge-stitching

Edge-stitching is similar to topstitching, but as the name implies, the sewn line parallels the edge of a fabric or project, often very closely.

Box-stitching

For joining handles, adding buckles, or any other seams that need some special reinforcement, I like to stitch a box with an X inside for added stability instead of using the standard topstitching. Just stitch a simple box shape, then at one corner, lift the sewing machine foot with the needle down, and, holding the fabric in place, pivot your project and stitch a diagonal line from corner to corner. Repeat to form an *X* shape (see fig. 5). Backstitch at the beginning and end of the box-stitching to reinforce.

Turning right-side out

Many sewing projects are created by stitching pattern pieces together on the wrong side of the fabric, leaving an opening, and then carefully turning the item right-side out. Here's how to do this (see figs. 6–9).

Press the fabric or patchwork pieces (in this figure, one of the Vintage Scarf Headband ties, page 31). Align them, right sides together and matching edges, and pin around the perimeter, leaving an opening as described in the project or marked on the paper pattern.

fig. 6

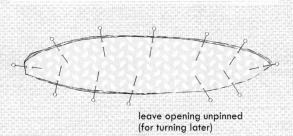

leave opening unpinned
(for turning later)

Stitch around the perimeter of the project using the appropriate seam allowance, backstitching at the beginning and end of your seams to secure them, and leaving the opening unsewn. Clip any corners close to the seam, but not through the stitch line. This will make the corners neater and easier to turn.

fig. 7

clip corners

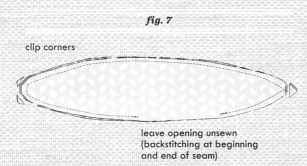

leave opening unsewn
(backstitching at beginning
and end of seam)

Gently turn the project right-side out through the opening, carefully pushing the corners out with a chopstick or pencil. Press it neatly. Fold and press the raw edges of the opening to the wrong side of the fabric, making sure to align the folded edges, and pin the opening closed. If the seam allowance was ¼ in/6 mm (as in this example), also fold the fabric raw edges under ¼ in/6 mm.

fig. 8

turned right side out
and pressed

raw edges of
opening folded
and pinned under

Topstitch or edge-stitch around the perimeter of your project, backstitching at the beginning and end to hold the seam, and stitching the opening securely closed.

fig. 9

topstitched around perimeter, backstitching to hold seam

Box corners

Use box corners (see figs. 10–12) to create a wide, generously sized base for a bag, instead of the flat envelope style you'd get by simply joining two pieces of fabric together. You'll use this technique in projects like the Cute-as-a-Button Handbag (page 121), Nesting Canisters (page 49), and Beach Tote Bag (page 71).

1. After joining the exterior bag, lining, or canister fabrics with a vertical side seam, press the project, front and back. Then, working on the wrong side of the fabric, fold the seam corner flat so it forms a triangle, and press it neatly, pressing your seam allowance to one side.

2. Use a quilt ruler and fabric marker or pin to mark the correct measurement of your box corner (in this illustration, 3 in/7.5 cm). Stitch the corner as shown, backstitching at the beginning and end of the seam to secure it.

fig. 10

3 in/7.5 cm

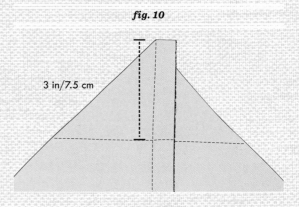

3. Using a rotary cutter and quilt ruler, trim the triangle away from the box corner, ¼ to ⅜ in/6 mm to 1 cm from the seam, as shown (see fig. 11). You can also zigzag stitch the raw edge for extra security, if you like.

fig. 11

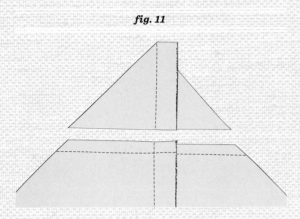

4. Gently turn the fabric right-side out, carefully pushing out the box corners with a chopstick or pencil (see fig. 12; unless the lining is meant to stay wrong-side out, see "Inserting a lining," following).

fig. 12

BOX CORNER

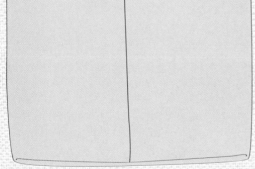

Inserting a lining

To insert a lining, first sew and press the exterior and lining pieces.

1. Place the lining into the exterior bag (or other project, such as a nesting canister), matching side seams, and with wrong sides facing.

2a. To finish with simple topstitching (like in the Cute-as-a-Button Handbag, page 121): fold and press the top raw edges of the lining to the wrong side, toward the bag they're tucked into (see fig. 13). Then fold and press the raw edges of the exterior fabric toward the lining. Pin the lining into the bag, including any handles or other elements (like the triangular bag closure for the Cute-as-a-Button Handbag). Edge-stitch around the perimeter of the bag opening, catching both lining and outer fabrics evenly.

fig. 13

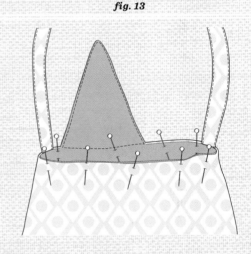

2b. To finish with binding around the raw edges of the exterior and lining pieces: pin the lining into the exterior piece, wrong sides facing. Edge-stitch around the perimeter of the opening, catching both layers. Then cover the opening with a joined ring of binding tape, pinning it securely in place, and including any handles (such as in the Mason Jar Cozy, page 115; see fig. 14, page 20). Machine-stitch the binding in place (see "Binding," page 20, for more detailed instructions), covering the raw edges of the joined lining and exterior pieces.

fig. 14

side of the fabric. Continue sewing the button down with at least three or four additional stitches through the holes until it is secure. If you have a four-hole button, you can stitch it down with either an *X* shape or two parallel stitches. For a shank button, simply bring your needle and thread from the back of the fabric through to the front, guide your needle through the shank, stitch back down from the front to the back of your fabric, and repeat for at least four stitches until it is secure. Knot your thread at the back to finish.

Sewing on a snap

To hand-sew a snap, thread a needle and knot it securely. Moving around the perimeter of one half of the snap set, use small, even stitches to secure it to the fabric (see fig. 15). Finish by knotting behind the snap securely. Then stitch the other half of the snap onto the corresponding place of your project in the same way. You can often cover the back of a snap with a decorative button.

Binding

Edge your projects with a neatly stitched fold of fabric for a clean, crisp finish. You can add binding to small projects like placemats and book covers as well as full-size quilts, in matching or contrasting fabrics.

Make your own binding tape: Though you can buy premade binding tape at a fabric store, I love to make custom binding with my own fabrics. For the projects in this book, cut binding on the straight or cross grain of the fabric rather than on the bias (bias tape is used for stretching around curves or garment holes to bind the edges).

1. To make 1-in/2.5-cm binding, the size used in this book, which can be folded into ½-in/12-mm double-folded binding tape, cut 2-in-/5-cm-wide strips of fabric with a quilt ruler and rotary cutter. You can cut strips on the cross grain, which is across the width of the fabric from selvage to selvage (useful for binding a quilt or larger project). Or you can cut strips along the straight grain line of a shorter length of fabric if you don't need as much (for a smaller project like a Nesting Canister, page 49, or the Sketchbook Cover, page 91).

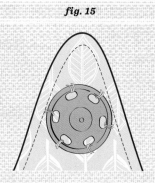

fig. 15

Sewing on a button

To hand-sew a button, thread a needle and knot it securely. Place the button in the correct spot on your project, and bring the needle and thread from the wrong side of the fabric and up through the first hole in the button and then down through the second hole, pulling the stitch taut; the knot is hidden on the wrong

2. To join more than one strip of fabric, place two strips right sides together, matching the short ends (see fig. 16A). Trim any selvages. Pin or hold the pieces together at the edge and stitch them with a ¼-in/6-mm seam allowance, backstitching at the beginning and end to hold the seam (see fig. 16B). Press the seam open (see figs. 16C and D), and continue to join as many strips of fabric as needed for your project.

3. Cut one end of your 2-in/5-cm strip at an angle and use a straight pin or the tip of a seam ripper to pull it through the 1-in/2.5-cm binding tape maker.

4. As you pull the fabric strip continuously through the binding tape maker (see fig. 17A), press it with an iron to create folded tape, with the raw edges of fabric pressed toward the center of the strip.

5. When you reach any joined seams, you may need to carefully ease them through the binding tape maker, and then press them open again.

6. After creating your folded, flat 1-in/2.5-cm binding (see fig. 17B), fold it again in half lengthwise to create ½-in/12-mm double-folded binding tape (see fig. 17C). Simply press it with an iron, moving along the length of the tape, to make a neat, straight fold. The raw edges will be hidden deep inside the fold.

fig. 16

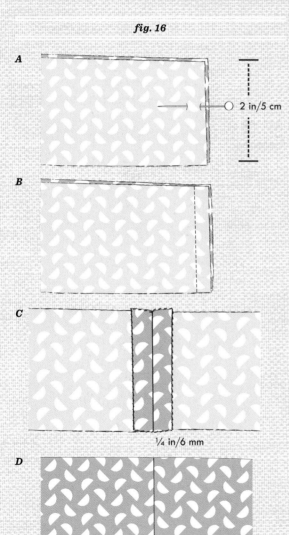

A

2 in/5 cm

B

C

¼ in/6 mm

D

fig. 17

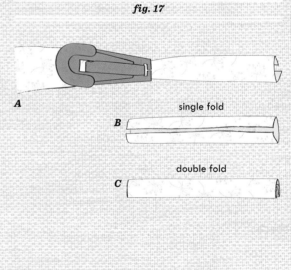

A

single fold

B

double fold

C

Attach the binding:

I originally learned this simple machine-binding method from Weeks Ringle and Bill Kerr's wonderful book *The Modern Quilt Workshop* (see Resources). I use it to quickly add binding to my quilts, bags, canisters, and other patchwork projects. It gets much easier with a little practice! If you prefer another binding method, of course you can use that one instead.

1. To machine-bind, first pin your double-folded binding tape in place (see fig. 18). I recommend edge-stitching around the perimeter of your project pieces first, so your project layers are neatly aligned in place. Arrange your binding so it encloses and hugs the edge of your project, folded neatly around both sides, and evenly distributed on the front and back. Pin it every 4 in/10 cm or so to keep it in place.

2. If you are edging something on only one side, like the top of a pocket for the Gardening Apron (page 37) or the flap of the Sketchbook Cover (page 91), simply stitch the binding down from one end to the other along the edge. At the ends, you can either fold the short raw ends of the tape under, or catch them within a seam (like for the Sketchbook Cover), depending on the project.

3. For a quilt or larger patchwork project (like a place-mat), I usually start binding along the bottom edge, where the final joining seam won't be as noticeable. Pin the binding tape in place, starting near the center and extending to the corner (see fig. 18). Start stitching about 5 in/12 cm from the raw-edge end of the binding; stitch it down very close to its inner folded edge, stopping ¼ in/6 mm from the corner. Backstitch to hold the seam in place. If you go over on either side, you can always do a quick seam ripping and repinning to resew it there.

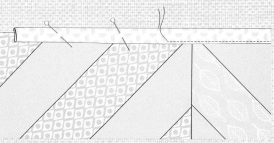

fig. 18

4. Press the binding tape at the corner, making a neat triangle (see fig. 19), and fold it back over the raw edge, catching and covering the end of the first seam you sewed. Pin the binding in place down the second side of the quilt or project.

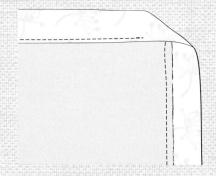

fig. 19

NOTE:

I hand-baste my corners before machine-sewing the next side of the binding, which helps make sure that the corner is neat and doesn't shift (see fig. 20). Use a bright contrasting thread color, make big stitches, and don't knot—then, when you're done, quickly remove the basting with scissors or a seam ripper. (See more detailed instructions for hand-basting on page 15.)

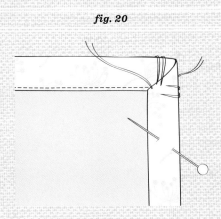

fig. 20

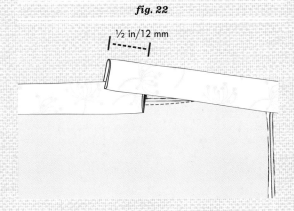

fig. 22

½ in/12 mm

5. Stitch from the first corner down the second side of your project (see fig. 21), backstitching to hold the seam. Stop stitching ¼ in/6 mm from the edge of the next corner.

8. Unfold both ends of the binding and pin them right sides together, short raw edges aligned. Stitch an exact ¼-in/6-mm seam to join the edges together (see fig. 23).

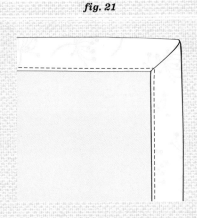

fig. 21

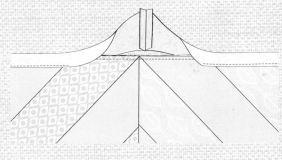

fig. 23

6. Continue sewing the binding until you have stitched all four corners and are nearing the beginning raw edge of the binding. Stop stitching about 6 in/15 cm from the beginning raw edge of the binding.

7. Carefully measure ½ in/12 mm beyond the beginning raw edge of the binding, and cut your working binding's edge to that point (see fig. 22).

9. Press the seam open, then re-press the folds of the binding back into place, and pin the binding around the edge. It should fit snugly. If the binding is too loose or too tight, open the seam and adjust the seam allowance, or stitch a new piece of binding onto the end of one strip and redo for a perfect, snug fit.

10. Sew the last few inches of binding, backstitching at the end of your seam (see fig. 24). Trim all threads and remove your basting stitches from corners.

fig. 24

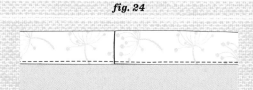

photo 1

BINDING VARIATIONS

Folded finish binding:

For a smaller project where joining the binding to finish would be too difficult (like a Patchwork Coaster, page 67, for example), I do a simple folded finish instead (see photo 1). Just stitch the binding down at the midpoint of the bottom edge, securing the whole length of binding to the first corner (instead of leaving the first part unsewn, to be joined later). Continue around the perimeter as previously instructed (see "Attach the binding," page 22). When you get to the bottom edge with the partly sewn binding, measure ¾ in/2 cm beyond the original binding start, and trim the new (working) binding tape to that point. Fold and press under ¼ in/6 mm and then pin the new folded-edge binding over the original, overlapping it by ½ in/12 mm and matching edges along the length. Sew it in place so that both the binding's raw ends are folded inside.

Binding along an opening:

To bind around or along the top of a bag, canister, or other small project, be sure to edge-stitch through all layers of the project, all the way around the perimeter, to keep the layers from shifting.

It's easiest to form a ring of binding and pin that right on to the project. Everyone stitches a little differently; I'll give my guidelines for creating the correct size of binding ring with each project, but you may want to check yours individually.

Pin the binding around the opening, and mark the overlap point. Trim your binding to ½ in/12 mm beyond that point, unpin the binding, unfold the short ends, and stitch the ends together with a ¼-in/6-mm seam allowance (see figs. 22 and 23, page 23). Press, repin the binding to the opening, and stitch it in place (see photo 2).

photo 2

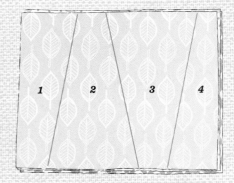

2. After you cut the fabrics, rearrange them into four different sets, from left to right. In this example, I'm using one of each fabric, with no repeats, to create a new 1, 2, 3, 4 arrangement (see fig. 26).

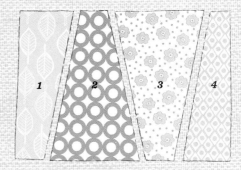

fig. 26

3. Once you like your four designs, stack your first arrangement in 1, 2, 3, 4 order and bring it to the sewing machine. Using a ¼-in/6-mm seam allowance, stitch 1 to 2 along the cutting line, right sides together. Repeat to join 3 to the other side of 2, and 4 to the other side of 3.

PATCHWORK

Stack and whack

This is a fun way to do a mix and match in patchwork: Stack your fabrics, make a simple series of angular cuts through all the layers, mix the fabrics up into new arrangements from one side to the other, then sew them back together! Here's how:

1. Stack your fabrics together (I used four) and use a fabric marker and quilt ruler to mark your three cutting lines (see fig. 25). Use a rotary cutter and quilt ruler to cut along all three lines. In this example, I'm making vertical cuts to divide each fabric into four pieces, 1, 2, 3, and 4.

4. Press all seams to one side. If you like, topstitch each seam, catching the pressed seam on the wrong side of the patchwork (see fig. 27).

fig. 27

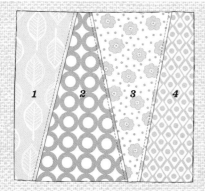

5. Repeat steps 3 and 4 to create your other three patchwork pieces. Use them to create a set of coasters, ornaments, or any other project you like!

String quilting

This simple piecing method yields a beautifully bold diagonal line within a quilt block or patchwork project. It's perfect for using scraps or "strings" of fabric left from other projects.

1. Cut a square of muslin exactly the size you want your quilt block or patchwork project to be. Press it. Arrange a pressed strip of fabric (that extends past the diagonal corners of the muslin) centered diagonally across the muslin, right-side up, pinning it in the center to hold it in place (see fig. 28A).

2. Place a second strip of fabric over the first, right sides together, aligning them along the long diagonal raw edge. Stitch through all layers with a ¼-in/6-mm seam allowance (see fig. 28B). Press the seams open, and trim both fabric strips close to the muslin square corner edges if they extend considerably beyond.

3. Align another strip of fabric along the opposite long raw edge, right sides together. Stitch through all layers with a ¼-in/6-mm seam allowance (see fig. 28C). Press the new strip of fabric open and trim it if needed.

4. Continue adding strips on both sides of the original center, working outward until the muslin block is filled with fabric strips (see fig. 28D). Press the block.

5. Flip the block over so you are looking at the back of the muslin (see fig. 28E).

6. Using a quilt ruler or square template and a rotary cutter, precisely trim off the excess fabric ends on all four sides of the muslin square (see fig. 28F).

7. Continue making string-pieced blocks the same way for potholders, trivets, quilts, or other patchwork projects. If you arrange four blocks together (as shown in fig. 28G), the diagonals form a striking diamond pattern! Join the blocks together with a ¼-in/6-mm seam allowance, matching edges and seams.

fig. 28

BASIC MACHINE QUILTING

Make a quilt sandwich with your backing fabric as a bottom layer, wrong side up, your batting smoothly arranged over it, and your patchwork/quilt top over the batting, right side up. For a larger project like the Picnic Quilt (page 77), be sure to use a larger batting and backing than quilt top, as described in the instructions; this doesn't matter as much with small projects that are well basted. (If you are using fusible batting on a smaller project like the Patchwork Potholders and Trivet [page 87], follow the manufacturer's instruc-tions to fuse it to the wrong side of your patchwork.) Baste the layers together with curved safety pins or large hand-basting stitches.

To quilt the layers, choose a pattern (straight lines are easiest for beginners) and mark your patchwork top with a washable fabric marker. Using a walking foot if you have one, simply stitch through all layers, along your marked lines from edge to edge. Finish by stitching the perimeter of the entire piece. See the Resources section (page 132) for many suggestions on books or classes to try more complex quilting options.

spring

Author
nesting canisters

Title
Denyse Schmidt (#1)

Date Due | **Borrower's Name** MMF
print
paired with "Aqua"

...gloss Products, Inc.

spring

Author
tri-fold sewing organizer

Title
deer print + gingham

Date Due | **Borrower's Name**
paired with MMF "Canary"
possibly contrast
color

pockets
contrast
with
outer +
lining

space for
needles,
pincushion,
scissors, thread,
...ucts, Inc. floss + small
projects

SPRING

VINTAGE SCARF HEADBAND

I collect vintage scarves, and I love wearing them in my hair. But the silky ones are hard to keep in place; they usually start sliding around a bit, even when anchored with bobby pins. I designed this simple headband with this problem in mind. It has long, flowy ties, inspired by one of my favorite Vera scarves, and it hides a very practical loop of elastic that helps it stay put. To personalize yours, use a favorite print in pretty colors—maybe to match a bag or a skirt!

DIMENSIONS:
Approx. 42 in/107 cm from end to end

TECHNIQUES USED:
Pattern tracing (page 14)
Seams (page 16)
Turning right-side out (page 17)
Topstitching (page 16)

PATTERNS NEEDED:
Vintage Scarf Headband and Vintage Scarf Headband Ties patterns (page 136)

Materials:

⅓ yd/0.3 m print fabric

Coordinating thread

10 in/25 cm flat elastic

Tools:

Pattern paper and pencil

Paper scissors

Fabric scissors

Pins

Sewing machine

Iron

Continued →

1. Enlarge and trace the Vintage Scarf Headband patterns onto the pattern paper with your pencil, marking the openings on your patterns, and cut out with the paper scissors. Using the fabric scissors, cut out two of the headband pattern and four of the ties pattern from your fabric and press each piece. Separate your four tie pieces into two pairs.

2. Pin your two headband pieces, right sides together, and stitch each long side, with a ¼-in/6-mm seam allowance, leaving the two ends open, as marked on the pattern. Turn the headband right-side out, press, and topstitch both long sides, leaving a 1-in/2.5-cm opening at each end.

3. Pin your first set of ties right sides together. Stitch them together with a ¼-in/6-mm seam allowance, leaving an opening as marked. Turn right-side out, pushing out the end corners with a chopstick or pencil if necessary. Fold and press the raw edges under at the opening and press entire tie piece flat. Topstitch around tie,

⅛ in/3 mm from the edge, making sure to close the opening. Repeat this step on the second set of tie pieces.

4. Carefully fold and use the iron to press the raw edges under ¼ in/6 mm on one end of the headband, and gently tuck the blunt end of one tie inside. Position the piece of elastic over the end of the tie, with about 1 in/2.5 cm of the elastic tucked inside the headband, and pin it in place (see fig. 1).

5. Topstitch this end of the headband closed, backstitching at beginning and end of the seam to secure (see fig. 2).

6. Repeat steps 4 and 5 with the other end of the headband and second tie, but while the headband, elastic, and tie are still pinned, try the headband on for comfort. (I left about 7 in/17 cm of my elastic showing between the two edges of the headband.) Once you are happy with the elastic tightness, topstitch all layers securely to finish your headband!

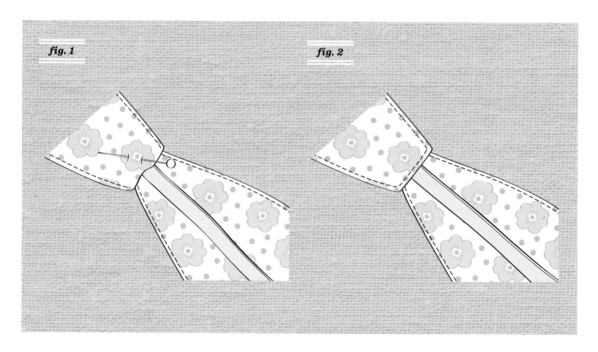

fig. 1

fig. 2

CAFÉ CURTAINS

This simple set of café curtains with contrasting binding at the top is perfect for fancying up a plain window. You can use an eyelet fabric with a decorative edge, like the curtains shown in this project, or trim a standard fabric with lace or another pretty extra. I glued small buttons on my curtain rings to match the soft pink of my eyelet fabric—totally optional, but cute!

DIMENSIONS: variable

TECHNIQUES USED:
Cutting without a pattern (page 14)
Binding (page 20)

Materials:

1 to 1½ yd/1 to 1.5 m fabric (amount depending on size of your windows), for curtains

¼ yd/0.25 m contrasting fabric, for binding

Coordinating thread

1 to 1½ yd/1 to 1.5 m trim, lace, or binding for hemming, if your fabric doesn't have a decorative edge (optional)

10 clip-on curtain rings

10 sew-through (flat) buttons (optional)

Tools

Tape measure

Rotary cutter, cutting mat, and quilt ruler

1-in/2.5-cm binding tape maker

Pins

Iron

Sewing machine

Hot glue gun (optional)

Continued ➜

1. Measure your window with the tape measure, and decide how tall and wide you want your curtains to be. Café curtains are decorative and usually just cover the bottom or central section of a larger window, instead of the whole area, like substantial drapes would. For my kitchen window, which measures 38 in/97 cm high and 48 in/122 cm wide from one side of the frame to the other, I wanted to make two curtains, each measuring 24 in/61 cm wide. Add 2¼ in/5.5 cm of width to that number to account for side hems and ease. I chose to make my curtains 18 in/46 cm tall. You won't need to account for any added height, since you'll use binding on the top, and you can make up for any hem length lost at the bottom by adding decorative trim. Write down your window and curtain measurements for reference.

WIDTH OF YOUR WINDOW: _____

÷ 2 = _____

+ 2¼ IN/5.5 CM

= WIDTH TO CUT EACH CURTAIN PANEL: _____

2. Using the rotary cutter, cutting mat, and quilt ruler, cut the fabric accordingly to create two curtains: Using my measurements, I cut two pieces 18 in/46 cm tall by 26 in/66.5 cm wide. Also cut 2-in/5-cm strips of your contrasting fabric, and use the binding tape maker to create double-folded binding tape the total width of your two curtains (for mine, 52 in/133 cm total).

3. Pin the binding over the raw edge at the top of one curtain piece and stitch it down. Trim it flush with both sides. Repeat this step on the second curtain piece.

4. If you're using a plain fabric (not one with a pre-finished decorative edge), turn and use the iron to press the lower edge of the fabric ¼ in/6 mm to the wrong side. Fold it under again ⅜ in/1 cm and press and pin in place. Stitch the double-folded hem securely in place. If you'd like to add a decorative lace or trim to the bottom of your curtains, hand- or machine-stitch it on over each hem, on the right side of the fabric. Repeat on the second curtain piece.

5. Turn and press the two vertical sides of your first curtain under ¼ in/6 mm to the wrong side of the fabric. Turn it under again ⅜ in/1 cm to hide the folded raw edge and pin in place, catching the end of the binding at the top and trim (if using) at the bottom. Stitch both pinned side seams from top to bottom, backstitching at the beginning and end of each seam to secure. Repeat to finish your second curtain.

6. If you'd like to embellish your curtain rings, hot glue a flat button to each one (following the manufacturer's instructions) and let them dry completely.

7. Clip five curtain rings onto the top of each curtain for hanging them: First clip a ring at the center and one at each end of one curtain. Then fold the curtain in half and put a clip between the center and edge on both sides, so the curtain hangs evenly. Repeat for the second curtain.

GARDENING APRON

This cute little three-pocket apron holds all the little things you reach for while gardening. Best of all, it easily slides from front to back when you need to get it out of the way for leaning forward. Edge a sturdy, utilitarian canvas in a solid color with a cheerful spring print that's as pretty as it is practical (just throw it in the washing machine when it gets muddy!).

DIMENSIONS:
9 by 20 in/23 by 51 cm

TECHNIQUES USED:
Pattern tracing (page 14)
Cutting without a pattern (page 14)
Seams (page 16)
Binding (page 20)
Edge-stitching (page 17)
Topstitching (page 16)
Box-stitching (page 17)

NOTE:

This project is very simple, but you'll customize the waistband length with your own measurements. Just measure around your waist, where you'd like to wear the apron (high at your natural waist, usually the smallest measurement of your midsection, or at your low waist, more toward your hips—it's up to you). Add 10 in/25 cm to that number, to create ends that will be sewn to the buckle. That's how long you should make the waistband, so it's adjustable and comfortable. Of course, you can add more length if you'd like to.

YOUR COMFORTABLE WAIST MEASUREMENT:
_____ + 10 in/25 cm = Waistband length: _____

Continued ➔

Materials:

½ yd/0.5 m medium-weight canvas, denim, or other home dec fabric (54 in/137 cm or wider)

¼ yd/0.25 m quilting cotton or other printed fabric (44 in/112 cm wide), for binding

Coordinating thread

1½ in/4 cm slide-release buckle

Tools:

Rotary cutter, cutting mat, and quilt ruler

Tape measure

1-in/2.5-cm binding tape maker

Pins

Sewing machine

Fabric marker

Iron

1. Using the rotary cutter, cutting mat, and quilt ruler, cut your fabrics.

CANVAS:

For the apron body and front pocket: Cut a 9-by-20-in/23-by-50-cm rectangle for the apron body, and a 7-by-22-in/17-by-56-cm rectangle for the pocket that goes across the front. Press each of these.

For the waistband: Follow the instructions in the Note for figuring your total waistband length. Cut a 3½-in-/9-cm-wide strip of canvas to that length. You can join two or more pieces of fabric together with a ½-in/12-mm seam allowance, if necessary, to get the desired length for your waistband piece.

COTTON:

For the binding: Cut 2-in-/5-cm-wide strips to total 64 in/163 cm, joining them as instructed for binding tape (see page 20). Using the binding tape maker, create ½-in-/12-mm-wide double-folded binding tape.

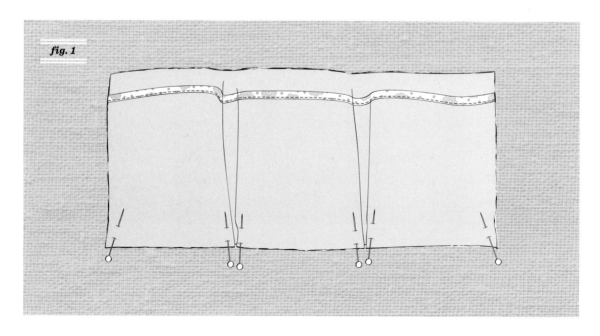

fig. 1

2. Pin the binding tape across one long edge of the front pocket piece (this will now be the top edge of the front pocket) and stitch it down to enclose the raw edge. Trim the ends of the binding so they're even with the pocket sides.

3. Using a fabric marker, draw a straight line 7 in/ 17 cm in from each of the short sides of the apron body piece, from top to bottom. The center section will be slightly smaller than the side sections. Now draw a straight line 7½ in/19 cm in from each of the short sides of the apron front pocket piece, also from top to bottom.

4. Align the front pocket piece over the body piece, right-sides up, aligning the bottom edges and the marks from step 3, and pinning at each of the marked lines. Stitch through both layers, from the bottom to the top of the front pocket piece, along both of the marked lines—this will separate the front pocket piece into three sections—backstitching at the beginning and end of the seam to secure. The front pocket sections will bubble up instead of lie flat: The front pocket piece has ease included, because it is a bit wider than the apron body piece.

5. Fold the extra front pocket fabric into pleats, and pin your pleats neatly, so there's a ¼-in/6-mm fold on each side of the two front pocket seams (see fig. 1). Press with the iron. The pleats create a roomier pocket that can hold more. Align and pin together the left and right raw side edges of the front pocket and apron body pieces, and edge-stitch along each raw side edge.

6. Starting on one short side, pin and stitch binding tape along the edge of the apron body, enclosing the raw edges of the apron body piece. Make a folded corner in the binding at the bottom and continue pinning and stitching to edge both sides and the bottom of the apron with binding tape. Leave the top raw edge of the apron piece unsewn.

7. Prepare your waistband: Press your 3½-in-/9-cm-wide strip. Fold and press ¼ in/6 mm under on both long raw edges to the wrong side. Then fold the waistband in half lengthwise, matching the folded edges together and creating a 1½-in-/4-cm-wide waistband. Use a tight zigzag stitch to "seal" both short ends, then topstitch the first 5 in/12 cm of the matched edges closed with a straight stitch.

8. Slip this sewn waistband section into the fixed half of the slide-release buckle and fold the short edge over about 2 in/5 cm, pinning it in place but leaving the buckle a little room to move. Box-stitch to hold it securely (see fig. 2).

Continued →

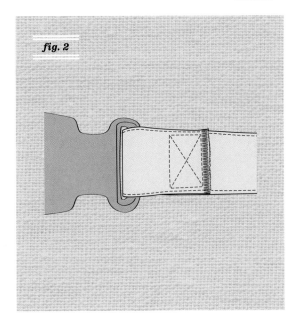

fig. 2

9. It might be handy to have a friend (or at least a mirror) around for the final placement. Wrap the waistband around you, where you want it to sit on your body. Place the buckle at the center of your back with the zigzagged edge toward your body (instead of facing outward). With a fabric marker or pin, mark the center front of the waistband (at your belly button). Then fold the apron piece in half, matching the short ends, and mark the top edge along the center fold. Tuck the top edge of the apron all the way to the top fold of the waistband, matching the center marks, and pin it in place. Begin topstitching the open (lower) edge of the waistband from the buckle end to the opposite end of the waistband. Topstitch the top (folded) edge of the waistband in the same way.

10. Slip the other half of the buckle onto the long edge of the waistband, try the apron on, and adjust it to a comfortable spot.

spring

Author

gardening apron

Title

green home dec

Date Due   Borrower's Name

edged with urban
chix floral
bias tape

practical
+
pretty-
pockets
buckle instead   for tools
of tie so it   & gloves
can easily move
to the back for active gardening

SPRING FLOWERS WRAP SKIRT

This light, pretty, and versatile skirt is perfect for those first warm and sunny spring days. It is surprisingly easy to make, too: no darts, no zipper, and no buttonholes. Once you figure out your size, simply join as many panels as you need for your base skirt—plus an overlap—and finish it with a neat twill-tape hem and waistband. French seams, twill tape, and a bit of zigzag stitching keep the inside finish neat, with no raw edges to deal with!

DIMENSIONS:
22 in/56 cm long; width is variable depending on size

TECHNIQUES USED:
Pattern drafting (see step 1)
French seams
(see steps 6 and 7)
Binding (page 20)
Sewing on a snap
(page 20; optional)

PATTERN NEEDED:
Skirt panel pattern
(see step 1)

NOTE:

This pattern fits like a puzzle for cutting. The diagonal lines align together so there is no fabric wasted between panels. Since you'll be cutting panels from folded fabric, some will be oriented the opposite way from others, so I recommend choosing a nondirectional print for this project. Florals or other "scattered" prints, solids, and small prints will work well.

Materials:

1¼ to 2 yd/1.25 to 2 m quilting cotton fabric (44 in/112 cm wide), for skirt

6 to 8 yd/5.5 to 7.5 m twill tape (2 in/5 cm wide) in a complementary color, for binding and waistband ties

Coordinating thread

Snap (optional)

Continued →

Tools:

- Quilt ruler and pencil
- Pattern paper
- Paper scissors
- Pins
- Fabric scissors
- Rotary cutter and cutting mat
- Tape measure
- Iron
- Sewing machine
- Seam ripper

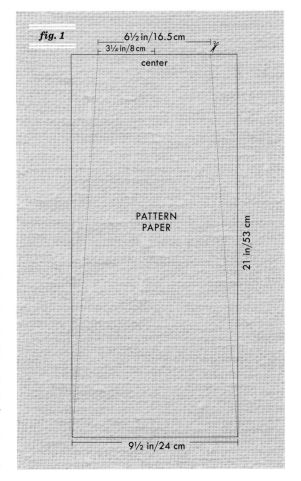

fig. 1

6½ in/16.5 cm

3¼ in/8 cm

center

PATTERN PAPER

21 in/53 cm

9½ in/24 cm

1. First, you'll create your skirt panel pattern. Using a quilt ruler and pencil, mark and cut a 21-by-9½-in/53-by-24-cm rectangular piece of pattern paper with the paper scissors. Place a pin at the center point of the top short edge. Mark 3¼ in/8 cm away from that center point on either side for a total width of 6½ in/16.5 cm: This will be the waist edge of the panel. Using the quilt ruler, draw a straight line between the top left mark on the waist edge and the left bottom corner of the pattern paper, and cut away the excess. Repeat on the right side (see fig. 1).

Continued ➜

MEASUREMENTS TABLE

Your comfortable waist measurement: _____ + 8 in/20 cm = long tie length: _____

PANELS NEEDED: Waist measurement:	23–27 in/ 58–69 cm	28–33 in/ 71–84 cm	34–38 in/ 86–97 cm	39–44 in/ 99–112 cm	45–50 in/ 114–127 cm
Base skirt panels:	4	5	6	7	8
+ Overlap panels:	3	3	3	3	3
Total panels to cut:	7	8	9	10	11

2. Take your comfortable waist measurement with a tape measure and write it in the Measurements Table. Using this number and the table, figure out how many panels you'll need to build your skirt. The final number of panels includes a certain number to fit your waist size for the "base skirt" plus a standard overlap of three more panels for the wrap. If you are between sizes or in doubt, you can generally size down to the next size range.

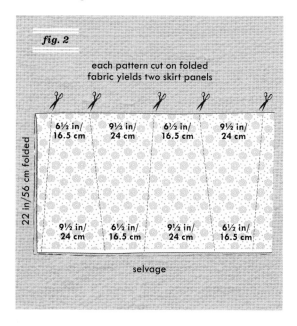

fig. 2

each pattern cut on folded fabric yields two skirt panels

22 in/56 cm folded

| 6½ in/ 16.5 cm | 9½ in/ 24 cm | 6½ in/ 16.5 cm | 9½ in/ 24 cm |

| 9½ in/ 24 cm | 6½ in/ 16.5 cm | 9½ in/ 24 cm | 6½ in/ 16.5 cm |

selvage

3. Fold your fabric in half, matching selvages. Place your skirt panel pattern at one end, so the narrower (6½-in/16.5-cm) end is along the fold and the wider end is near (or at) the selvage edge of the folded fabric (see fig. 2). Pin the pattern in place, and using fabric scissors, or a rotary cutter and quilt ruler, cut along both long sides of your pattern. Since you cut through two layers of fabric, this yields your first two skirt panels (#1 and #2). If the selvage extends beyond your panel pattern, trim it away. Otherwise, it will be hidden inside the twill tape waistband and hem.

4. Unpin the pattern from the first two-panel cut, and set those pieces aside. Flip the pattern so the opposite end is along the fold of the fabric, and pin the pattern to the next section of fabric. Match the diagonal cut edge of the fabric to the diagonal edge of the pattern. Cut the second two-panel (#3 and #4). Continue to cut more skirt panels, flipping the pattern before each cut, until you have the total number you need for your skirt. If you need an odd number of panels, you can unfold your fabric and cut the last panel as a single instead of a pair.

5. Each pair of skirt panels will still be joined at the fabric fold. Use fabric scissors or a rotary cutter to separate them. Press all panels with the iron.

6. Now you'll join each skirt panel with French seams. Stack your first two panels (#1 and #2) together, matching all raw edges, with the fabric wrong sides together. Stitch them together along one long (21-in/53-cm) edge with a ¼-in/6-mm seam allowance (see fig. 3A). It may seem strange to sew fabric with the right sides facing out, but you'll see the raw edges of this seam disappear in a minute!

7. Press the ¼-in/6-mm seam to one side, then fold the fabric along the seam so that the right sides are now facing together and press the fabric again along the seam. Now the raw edges of the seam allowance are neatly hidden inside the fold. Then stitch the panels together with a ⅜-in/1-cm seam allowance along the seamed edge, catching the narrower, first seam within (see fig. 3B). Press your French seam to one side (see fig. 3C).

Continued ➔

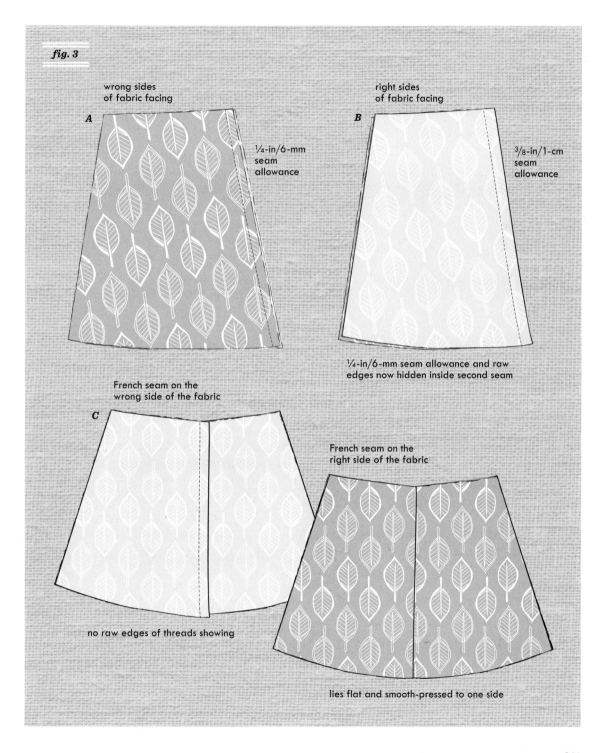

fig. 3

wrong sides
of fabric facing

A

¼-in/6-mm
seam
allowance

right sides
of fabric facing

B

⅜-in/1-cm
seam
allowance

¼-in/6-mm seam allowance and raw
edges now hidden inside second seam

French seam on the
wrong side of the fabric

C

no raw edges of threads showing

French seam on the
right side of the fabric

lies flat and smooth-pressed to one side

NOTE

This project uses French seams to connect
the skirt panels, as described on page 45.
This doubled seam makes a beautifully
neat join, since the raw edges are hidden
deep inside a second, wider seam. This
version of the French seam adds up to a
⅝-in/16-mm seam allowance (¼ in/6 mm
+ ⅜ in/1 cm per seam), which is a standard
in American garment making. See fig. 3C
for how the seam looks on the right and
wrong sides of the fabric.

11. Using a zigzag stitch, neatly machine-sew all along the V to secure it (see fig. 4).

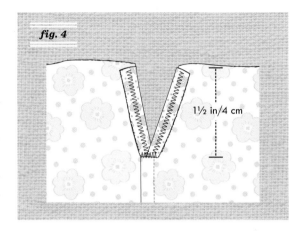

fig. 4

1½ in/4 cm

8. Sew panel #3 to the right side of your first two joined pieces in the same way, to continue building your skirt. Make sure that waist edges (6½-in/16.5-cm edges) are all placed along the same side each time you add a panel. Add panels until your skirt is wide enough to wrap around your body, but with no overlap yet—it just meets (or almost meets) at the waist. This is your base skirt.

9. Now add the last three panels (the overlap) to your base skirt. Stitch them on the same way, adding them to the left side of the base skirt when looking at the inside of the skirt. Mark the join between the base and the last three overlap panels with a pin. Also, along the join you've just marked, measure down 1½ in/4 cm from the top edge (waist) and mark that spot with a pin.

10. Using a seam ripper, carefully open both layers of your French seam to the marked point (1½ in/4 cm down) in order to create a small V opening, or gap, keeping the fabric folded as it was for the original two seams. This gap will become the opening you'll thread the wrap skirt tie through for cinching your skirt snug around your waist. Press the V back and front, making sure the raw edges are folded under.

12. Press your wrap skirt front and back. Trim any small points or angles from your French seams so the waist and hem are relatively smooth, and press each seam in the same direction.

13. Press the 2-in/5-cm twill tape so it's neatly folded in half lengthwise, finishing so it's 1-in/2.5-cm wide. Looking at the inside (French seams showing) of your skirt, pin the folded tape over the right-side edge. Starting at the top, stitch it down one side of the skirt (see fig. 5), catching the raw edges of the skirt inside the twill tape "binding," and backstitching at the beginning and end of the seam to secure.

14. At the end of that side edge, make a folded corner with the twill tape (see Binding, page 20), pin it in place, and then pin the twill tape along the bottom raw edge of the skirt to form a hem, sandwiching the bottom of each pressed French seam inside. Stitch it in place.

15. At the end of the bottom hem, make another folded corner, and pin the twill tape up the left side of the skirt. Stitch it down, and trim it flush with the skirt waist edge.

16. You're almost done! Now you'll add your twill tape waistband ties. Like calculating your number of skirt panels for a custom fit, you'll need to do a little math to make sure your waist ties are the right length. Your short tie length, the one on the same side as your gap opening, will measure 22 in/56 cm. For the long tie length, add 8 in/20 cm to your waist measurement (from the Measurements Table) and fill in that number in the table as well: This will be the tie on the opposite side from the gap opening.

17. Pin the twill tape onto the top edge of the skirt, arranging it as shown in fig. 6, with the left side extending past the waist edge 22 in/56 cm to make the short tie and the right side extending past the waist edge the length you calculated in step 16 (your waist + 8 in/20 cm) to make the long tie. (You can always lengthen or shorten your ties if you prefer.) Fold, press, and pin under ¼ in/6 mm on each short end of your ties, and edge-stitch your entire waistband/ties tape along the bottom edge, up one short end, along the top edge, and back down the second short end. Backstitch at the beginning and end of the seam to secure.

18. Try on your skirt again, slipping the longer end of the tie through the *V* opening at the overlap point and wrapping it around your waist to tie at the side. If you'd like a little insurance against sudden spring breezes, mark a spot toward the bottom corner of the overlap and sew a snap on the inside of the wrap, and the outside of the base skirt underneath, in the corresponding spot. Snap your skirt closed for extra security!

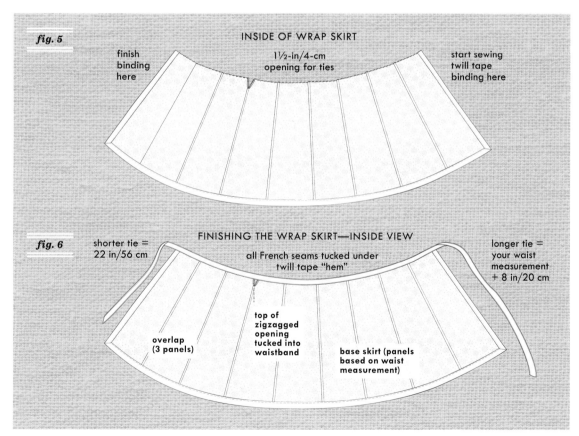

fig. 5

INSIDE OF WRAP SKIRT

finish binding here

1½-in/4-cm opening for ties

start sewing twill tape binding here

fig. 6

FINISHING THE WRAP SKIRT—INSIDE VIEW

shorter tie = 22 in/56 cm

all French seams tucked under twill tape "hem"

longer tie = your waist measurement + 8 in/20 cm

overlap (3 panels)

top of zigzagged opening tucked into waistband

base skirt (panels based on waist measurement)

NESTING CANISTERS

I love the pretty set of orange and yellow vintage flour, sugar, tea, and coffee canisters I have in my kitchen, a gift from my aunt. When it comes to organizing my sewing table, I always need good places to put special things—an ever-growing collection of printed selvages, a project in progress, or all the fabrics for this month's bee block. So I made some fabric "canisters" based on the vintage ones I adore so much. They're almost a cross between canister and bowl: wide enough to hold lots of things, but taller than they are broad so that they don't take up too much space. I've included dimensions and instructions for small, medium, and large versions. They look adorable all nested together!

DIMENSIONS:

Small canister: 5 in/12 cm tall

Medium canister:
6 in/15 cm tall

Large canister:
7½ in/19 cm tall

TECHNIQUES USED:

Cutting without a pattern
(page 14)

Rule of thirds patchwork
(see Note, page 50)

Seams (page 16)

Box corners (page 18)

Turning right-side out
(page 17)

Inserting a lining (page 19)

Edge-stitching (page 17)

Binding (page 20)

Topstitching (page 16)

Materials (for all three canisters):

¾ yard/0.7 m solid or print fabric (fabric A),
for exterior and lining

⅓ yard/0.3 m contrasting solid or print fabric
(fabric B), for the exterior panel and binding

Coordinating thread

½ yard/0.5 m heavyweight interfacing
(44 in/112 cm wide) (see Note, page 50)

½ or 1 yard/0.5 or 1 m fusible batting
(44 in/112 cm wide) (see Note, page 50)

Tools

Rotary cutter, cutting mat, and quilt ruler

Iron

Pins

Sewing machine

1-in/2.5-cm binding tape maker

Tape measure

Continued →

I backed my lining fabric with heavy-weight interfacing and my outer canister fabric with fusible batting. But my friend Pétra sewed a few sets of canisters backing both layers with batting and loved the results. Double layers of batting will create a soft but sturdy canister, while interfacing + batting gives a more rigid feel. It's up to you which version you'd rather make!

1. Using the rotary cutter, cutting mat, and quilt ruler, cut your fabrics.

FABRIC A:

For small canister: one 12-by-8-in/30.5-by-20-cm rectangle for lining and one 8-by-8-in/20-by-20-cm rectangle for exterior

For medium canister: one 16-by-10-in/40.5-by-25-cm rectangle for lining and one 12-by-10-in/30.5-by-25-cm rectangle for exterior

For large canister: one 20-by-12-in/50-by-30.5-cm rectangle for lining and one 16-by-12-in/40.5-by-30.5-cm rectangle for exterior

FABRIC B:

For small canister: two 2½-by-8-in/6-by-20-cm rectangles for exterior panel

For medium canister: two 2½-by-10-in/6-by-25-cm rectangles for exterior panel

For large canister: two 2½-by-12-in/6-by-30.5-cm rectangles for exterior panel

For all three canisters: 2-by-60-in/5-by-153-cm strip, for binding

INTERFACING:

(cut one each; or cut two each of fusible batting, if you prefer)

For small canister: 12-by-8-in/30.5-by-20-cm rectangle

For medium canister: 16-by-10-in/40.5-by-25-cm rectangle

For large canister: 20-by-12-in/50-by-30.5-cm rectangle

FUSIBLE BATTING:

For small canister: 12-by-8-in/30.5-by-20-cm rectangle

For medium canister: 16-by-10-in/40.5-by-25-cm rectangle

For large canister: 20-by-12-in/50-by-30.5-cm rectangle

NOTE:

The rule of thirds for patchwork is simple: dividing a design into thirds creates an appealing look (see photo on p. 48). I particularly like the arrangement of the top one-third being in one fabric or print, and the bottom two-thirds in a contrasting fabric or print. The ratio certainly doesn't have to be exact, but this general proportion looks really nice!

2. Press each piece with the iron. You'll assemble and sew each canister the same way.

3. For the three canisters, stitch each of the exterior panel pieces (fabric B) to each short end of your exterior pieces (fabric A), using a ¼-in/6-mm seam allowance. Press the seam allowance toward the darker of the two fabrics.

4. Following the package instructions, fuse the interfacing (or batting, if using) to the wrong side of your lining piece, and fuse the fusible batting to the wrong side of your exterior piece. Trim any excess interfacing or batting, and press.

5. Sew lining sides: Fold the lining in half widthwise, right sides together, align all edges, and pin each of the short sides together. Stitch pinned sides together with a ⅜-in/1-cm seam allowance, backstitching at beginning and end to secure the seam. Mark, fold, and stitch two box corners: Sew 1½ in/4 cm in from the tip of the triangle for the small canister, 2 in/5 cm in from the tip of the triangle for the medium, and 2½ in/6 cm in from the tip of the triangle for the large canister. Trim box corners.

6. Sew exterior fabric: Fold the exterior piece in half widthwise, right sides together, align all edges, and pin each of the short sides together. Make sure to match the contrasting fabric seams. Stitch pinned sides together with a ¼-in/6-mm seam allowance, backstitching at beginning and end to secure seam. Fold and stitch two box corners the same way as for the lining (step 5), and trim.

7. Gently turn exterior piece right-side out. Tuck lining inside, with wrong sides together, matching side seams, and pin around the top opening. The lining may show a little above the exterior. Edge-stitch around the top opening of the canister and trim any excess so both of the top edges are even.

8. Using the binding tape maker, create double-folded binding tape from the 2-in-/5-cm-wide strip you cut of fabric B. Measure around the top perimeter of each canister with a tape measure, and note that number. (My small canister measured 14½ in/37 cm, my medium 18½ in/47 cm, and my large 22½ in/57 cm, but small differences in sewing can occur, so measure your canisters' perimeters to be sure.) Cut the bind-

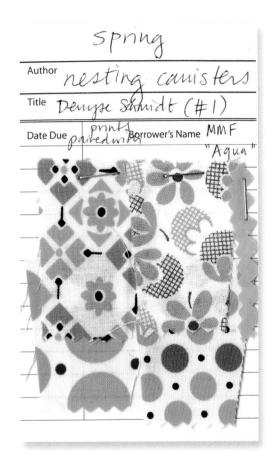

ing tape to this measurement plus ½ in/12 mm, and stitch the short ends together with a ¼-in/6-mm seam allowance. Pin the binding tape snugly onto the top of the canister, enclosing the raw edges. Topstitch the binding in place around the perimeter of the opening, exterior-side out.

SEWING ORGANIZER

by Michelle Freedman

Michelle Freedman, who designed this darling project, and I are members of the Portland Modern Quilt Guild. We host a big all-day sew every couple of months, where a few dozen of us get together to sew, chat, and shop for fabric. This handy tri-fold design is perfect for holding sewing and patchwork supplies you might bring to a sew day or take on a trip. You'll love all the pockets and details she included for keeping everything organized!

DIMENSIONS:

9 by 20 in/23 by 51 cm (open)

9 by 7 in/23 by 18 cm (closed)

TECHNIQUES USED:

Cutting without a pattern (page 14)

Seams (page 16)

Topstitching (page 16)

Rule of thirds patchwork (see Note, page 50)

Box-stitching (page 17)

Edge-stitching (page 17)

Binding (page 20)

Sewing on a button (page 20)

NOTE:

For a stiffer, sturdier organizer, you can reinforce the lining with a medium-weight fusible interfacing on the wrong side in Step 15.

Materials:

1/3 yd/0.3 m quilting cotton (44 in/112 cm wide), fabric A

1/3 yd/0.3 m quilting cotton (44 in/112 cm wide), fabric B

1/4 yd/0.25 m quilting cotton (44 in/112 cm wide), fabric C

3-by-4-in/7.5-by-10-cm felt scrap

3-by-4-in/7.5-by-10-cm fusible batting scrap

1½ yd/1.5 m twill tape (½ in/12 mm wide) (we used a measuring tape print)

Coordinating thread

9-by-20½-in/23-by-52-cm piece of fusible batting

11-by-22-in/28-by-56-cm piece of muslin or other lightweight fabric

4 in/10 cm elastic (½ in/12 mm wide)

2 in/5 cm Velcro (5/8 in/16 mm wide)

1/3 yard/0.3 m of medium-weight fusible interfacing (44 in/112 cm wide) (optional)

One 1⅜-in/3.5-cm button

Continued →

Tools:

Rotary cutter, cutting mat, and quilt ruler

Pinking shears

Sewing machine

Pins

Iron

1-in/2.5-cm binding tape maker

Hand-sewing needle

1. Using the rotary cutter, cutting mat, quilt ruler, and pinking shears, cut the fabrics:

FABRIC A:

One 9-by-14-in/23-by-35.5-cm rectangle, for exterior

Three 9-by-7-in/23-by-17-cm rectangles, for interior pockets and background

FABRIC B:

One 9-by-7-in/23-by-17-cm rectangle, for exterior

One 4-by-4½-in/10-by-11-cm rectangle, for a pocket

One 5½-by-4½-in/14-by-11-cm rectangle, for a pocket lining

One 9-by-14-in/23-by-35.5-cm rectangle, for interior

FABRIC C:

Three 2-in-/5-cm-wide fabric strips (one 9 in/23 cm long for the exterior, one 4½ in/11 cm long for a pocket section, and one 64 in/163 cm long for binding the perimeter)

One 3½-by-4½-in/9-by-11-cm rectangle (cut with pinking shears), for the pincushion background

FELT:

One 3-by-4-in/7.5-by-10-cm rectangle, for the pincushion

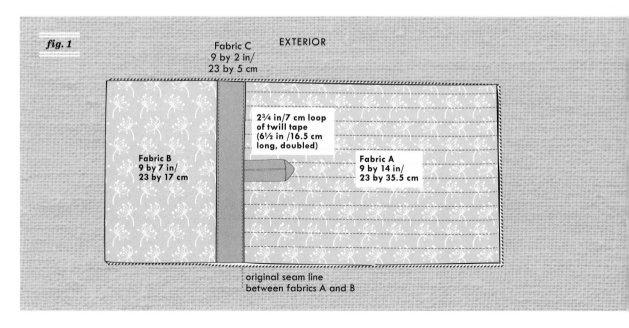

fig. 1

Fabric C
9 by 2 in/
23 by 5 cm

EXTERIOR

Fabric B
9 by 7 in/
23 by 17 cm

2¾ in/7 cm loop
of twill tape
(6½ in /16.5 cm
long, doubled)

Fabric A
9 by 14 in/
23 by 35.5 cm

original seam line
between fabrics A and B

TWILL TAPE:

> One 6½-in/16.5-cm piece, for the exterior tab
>
> One 15-in/38-cm piece, for a scissors or rotary cutter tie
>
> One 4-in/10-cm piece, for the interior tab
>
> Two 10-in/25-cm pieces, for holding threads

2. Construct the exterior of the organizer (see fig. 1). With right sides together, stitch the 9-by-14-in/23-by-35.5-cm rectangle of fabric A to the 9-by-7-in/23-by-17-cm rectangle of fabric B along the 9-in/23-cm sides, using a ¼-in/6-mm seam allowance. Fuse the now 9-by-20½-in/23-by-52-cm exterior piece to the fusible batting with the iron.

3. Place the fused exterior/batting piece over the muslin piece, pin, and quilt as desired. (Michelle used horizontal and vertical quilting lines, about ¾ in/2 cm apart. You can choose any style of quilting.) Trim away excess muslin.

4. Prepare the tab: Fold the 6½-in-/16.5-cm-long piece of twill tape into the tab loop (see fig. 1). Pin it in the center of the exterior piece seam (right-side up), tab toward fabric A, and a ½-in/12-mm seam allowance extending past the seam onto fabric B.

5. With the 9-in-/23-cm-long strip of fabric C, press ¼ in/6 mm under on both long sides. With right-side up, place the pressed strip over the tab, catching the raw edges of your twill tape underneath, and pin in place, matching the right edge of the strip to the seam you sewed in step 2. Topstitch along both long edges of the strip.

6. Construct the inner section of the organizer (see fig. 2). We'll start with the right-side "page" of the three pages in the organizer, which is built on one piece of 9-by-7-in/23-by-17-cm piece of fabric A.

Continued ➜

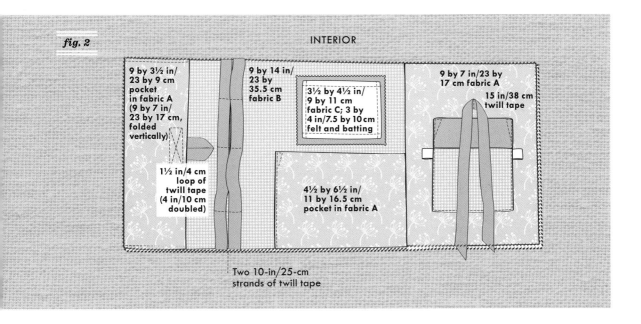

fig. 2   INTERIOR

9 by 3½/ 23 by 9 cm pocket in fabric A (9 by 7 in/ 23 by 17 cm, folded vertically)

9 by 14 in/ 23 by 35.5 cm fabric B

3½ by 4½ in/ 9 by 11 cm fabric C; 3 by 4 in/7.5 by 10 cm felt and batting

9 by 7 in/23 by 17 cm fabric A

15 in/38 cm twill tape

1½ in/4 cm loop of twill tape (4 in/10 cm doubled)

4½ by 6½ in/ 11 by 16.5 cm pocket in fabric A

Two 10-in/25-cm strands of twill tape

RIGHT "PAGE":

Build the front of your patch pocket (see fig. 3). With right sides together, stitch your 4-by-4½-in/10-by-11-cm piece of fabric B to the 2-by-4½-in/5-by-11-cm piece of fabric C, using a ¼-in/6-mm seam allowance. Press seams toward fabric C. Lay this joined fabric over the 5½-by-4½-in/14-by-11-cm piece of fabric B (the lining), right sides together. Sew around the perimeter of three of the sides, with a ¼-in/6-mm seam allowance, leaving the bottom (fabric B end) open. Clip the top two (sewn) corners and gently turn the pocket right-side out.

7. Mark ½ in/12 mm from the bottom (unsewn) edge of the pocket and fold it to the lining (underside) of the pocket. Cut the elastic piece in half, so you have two 2-in/5-cm pieces, then fold each of these pieces in half again. With right sides up, pin the pocket in place in the center of the "page," so the top edge of the pocket is 3 in/7.5 cm below the top of the page, tucking and pinning the two elastic loops into the two sides. Edge-stitch down all three sides of the pocket, reinforcing the two upper corners with stitched triangles. Press.

8. Make the notions tie. Mark the center of your 15-in/38-cm twill tape and stitch it down above the center of the patch pocket, 2 in/5 cm below the top edge.

LEFT "PAGE":

9. Prepare the vertical pocket for the left "page." Fold one piece of 9-by-7-in/23-by-17-cm piece of fabric A lengthwise, with wrong sides together, to form a 9-by-3½-in/23-by-8.5-cm pocket, and press. The pocket right side has the fold to the right; the pocket wrong side has the fold to the left. With the pocket wrong side up, mark the center of the fold edge. Prepare your 4-in/10-cm piece of twill tape by folding (see fig. 2, page 55) and overlapping raw edges of the twill tape over the center pocket fold by ½ in/12 mm. Center one side of the 2-in/5-cm strip of Velcro vertically, ¼ in/6 mm from the fold, and covering the edges of the twill tape. Pin in place and box-stitch around the Velcro strip.

10. Place the vertical pocket over the left edge of your 9-by-14-in/23-by-35.5-cm piece of fabric B, right-side up, and mark the corresponding place for the other half of the Velcro. Box-stitch it in place. Machine-baste

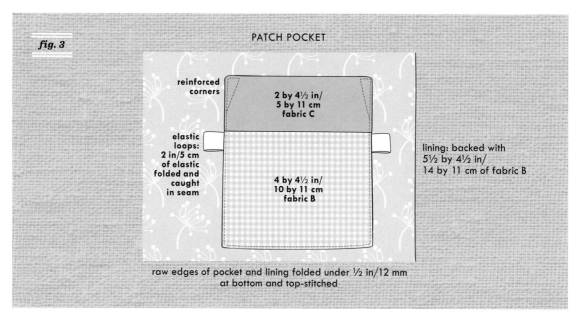

PATCH POCKET

fig. 3

reinforced corners

2 by 4½ in/ 5 by 11 cm fabric C

elastic loops: 2 in/5 cm of elastic folded and caught in seam

4 by 4½ in/ 10 by 11 cm fabric B

lining: backed with 5½ by 4½ in/ 14 by 11 cm of fabric B

raw edges of pocket and lining folded under ½ in/12 mm at bottom and top-stitched the pocket in place, along the three raw edges, ¼ in/ 6 mm from the edge.

11. Add the two 10-in/25-cm strips of twill tape, which will hold spools of thread or other notions. The strips will be parallel to each other, one placed 1¼ in/ 3 cm to the right of the vertical pocket and the other directly next to it on the right. Stitch both twill tapes down at the top, the bottom, and the center to fabric B, reinforcing the seam with backstitching. Michelle included ease in the strip measurements (like for the pockets of the Gardening Apron on page 37) so your twill tape will be longer than your base fabric.

12. Stitch both tapes down at the halfway point between the raw edges and center, alternating between adding ease and sewing flat (see photo, page 52).

CENTER "PAGE":
13. Prepare the horizontal pocket. Fold the remaining 9-by-7-in/23-by-17-cm piece of fabric A widthwise, right sides together, and gently press. On one short end, stitch a ¼-in/6-mm seam allowance (the right side of the rectangle if you are using directional fabric) from top to bottom, clip the top corner, and turn right-side out.

14. With right-sides up, match the raw bottom edge of the pocket to the bottom right 9-by-14-in/23-by-35.5-cm piece of fabric B, and the raw side edge of the pocket to the rightmost edge of fabric B. Edge-stitch the finished (left) side of the pocket, with a reinforced triangle at the top.

15. Layer the 3-by-4-in/7.5-by-10-cm piece of felt over the same-size piece of batting and fuse them together. Lay and center the felt-batting rectangle over the 3½-by-4½-in/9-by-11-cm pinked rectangle of fabric C. Place it above the horizontal pocket, 1 in/2.5 cm below the top edge of the center page, and edge-stitch onto the page around all four sides of the felt.

FINISH INTERIOR:
16. With right sides together, stitch the left and center pages to the right page, using a ¼-in/6-mm seam allowance, and catching the raw horizontal pocket edge within the seam. Press.

COMPLETE THE ORGANIZER:
17. Place the interior over the exterior, wrong sides together. Baste around the perimeter of the organizer, ¼ in/6 mm from the edge.

18. Using the binding tape maker, make double-folded binding tape with the 64-in/163-cm piece of fabric C, and bind the edges of the organizer (see page 20). Close the left and right pages over the center page.

19. Hand-stitch the button in place on the outside of the organizer with the needle and thread, centering it vertically (ours was 1½ in/4 cm from the finished edge), so it fits into the twill tape loop for closure.

Summer

Author Coasters & Placemats

Title paired with 4 MMF solids

1 stack whole patch-
work

Borrower's Name

LIGHT

"see"
napkins etc.

Products, Inc.

Summer

Author Solid fabric

Title coasters & pl

Date Due

Borrower's N

&
nice
with
prints!

cts, Inc.

SUMMER

Lansing PEARLS WASHABLE IN BUTTONS

Author: Summer (assorted pink + MMF "coral")
Title: picnic quilt 1" "tangerine"
"Sun" + "bright _____"
Date Due: string quilt with ~20
_____ fabrics

PORCH SWING PILLOWS

This cheerful pair of reversible pillows is perfect for a porch swing, to go with a picnic blanket, or for anywhere else you want to hang out to soak up the summer sun. Mixing a solid color with bright, graphic stripes of color is an easy way to bring in an instant visual pop—whether you pair solid pieces of the alternating fabrics back-to-back or stitch them into a wide striped panel pattern on each side. And using Velcro instead of an invisible zipper makes them even faster to whip up!

DIMENSIONS:
19 in/48 cm square

TECHNIQUES USED:
Cutting without a pattern (page 14)
Edge-stitching (page 17)
Seams (page 16)
Turning right-side out (page 17)
Stack and whack patchwork (for panel pillow) (page 25)
Rule of thirds patchwork (for panel pillow) (see Note, page 50)

Materials (for two pillows):
⅔ yd/0.6 m solid-color home dec fabric, fabric A

⅔ yd/0.6 m patterned home dec fabric, fabric B

1¼ yd/1.25 m sew-in Velcro (½ in/12 mm wide)

Coordinating thread

Two 18-in/46-cm square pillow forms

Tools:
Rotary cutter, cutting mat, and quilt ruler

Pins

Sewing machine

Iron

Continued →

Summer

Author

porch pillows

Title

agua paired with

Date Due | Borrower's Name

colorful stripes

color
blocking

wide
stripes

bright +
cheerful

SOLID-COLOR PILLOW COVER:

1. Using the rotary cutter, cutting mat, and quilt ruler, cut two 20-in/50-cm squares, one of fabric A and one of fabric B. Cut a 20-in/50-cm length of Velcro and then separate it into two halves. Pin one half of the Velcro along the bottom edge of each fabric, on the right side of the fabric, so the long edge of the Velcro is aligned exactly with the bottom edge of the fabric.

2. Starting at the bottom corner of fabric A, edge-stitch all four sides of the Velcro down to the first piece of fabric. Edge-stitch the second piece of Velcro to the second piece of fabric the same way.

3. Carefully (with a low iron setting, no steam, and pressing cloth, or following manufacturer's instructions, so the Velcro will not be damaged) fold and press the Velcro lengths toward the wrong side of the fabric, so they will eventually be hidden inside the pillow cover. Place the fabric A and fabric B squares, right sides together, and pin the other three sides of the fabric squares together.

4. Starting at one Velcro-folded edge, stitch the other three sides of the squares using a ½-in/12-mm seam allowance, backstitching at the beginning and end to secure the seam.

5. Clip the corners with the scissors, and turn the pillow cover right-side out. Try it on your pillow form. If it's too loose, turn it wrong-side out and restitch until it fits more closely. Insert the pillow form and close the Velcro.

PANEL PILLOW COVER:

6. Cut one 20-by-22-in/50-by-56-cm rectangle of fabric A and one of fabric B. Press them and stack them together. Using a rotary cutter and quilt ruler and a variation on the stack and whack method, cut the two fabrics into three rectangular sections: 20 by 7 in/ 50 by 17 cm (top), 20 by 8 in/50 by 20 cm (center), and 20 by 7 in/50 by 17 cm (bottom), so the design reflects the general rule of thirds patchwork arrangement.

7. Place the fabrics into A-B-A and B-A-B arrangements. Using a ½-in/12-mm seam allowance, join your A-B-A fabrics and then your B-A-B fabrics so they become two 20-in/50-cm squares of three fabric panels each.

8. Press the seams to one side (I pressed toward the striped fabric each time) and topstitch the seams.

9. Sew together the panel pillow cover the same way you did for the solid pillow cover, aligning the Velcro at the bottom along one continuous edge, not along the seamed panel sections, which will be the sides of the pillow cover. When you pin the fabrics together, match the side seams at each panel seam, and sew with a ½-in/12-mm seam allowance.

SUNGLASSES CASE

This cheerful little sunglasses case is just the thing to throw in your beach tote: a simple sleeve to protect your sunglasses from getting bounced around and scratched up. The case takes so little fabric that whether you're making a patchwork or whole-cloth version, you can easily sew a few from just a couple of fat quarters (a whole-cloth version), or a few strips of a jelly roll pack!

DIMENSIONS:
7 by 3½ in/17 by 9 cm

TECHNIQUES USED:
Pattern tracing (page 14)
Seams (page 16)
Turning right-side out (page 17)
Topstitching (page 16)

PATTERN NEEDED:
Sunglasses Case pattern (page 137)

NOTE:

"Jelly roll" strips are 2½-in-/6 cm-wide strips of fabric, usually cut the width of the material, and often including a designer's entire line—a fun and affordable way to use a whole collection. My patchwork version of this project uses small sections of four jelly roll strips. I used my friend and PMQG-mate Monica Solorio-Snow's Happy Mochi Yum Yum line for this cheerful patchwork case!

Materials:

One 8-by-9-in/20-by-23-cm piece fabric for the whole-cloth exterior, or four different 2½-by-9-in/6-by-23-cm strips fabric, for a patchwork exterior

One 8-by-9-in/20-by-23 cm piece fabric for the lining

One 8-by-9-in/20-by-23-cm piece fusible batting

Coordinating thread

Continued →

Tools:

- Pattern paper and pencil
- Paper scissors
- Rotary cutter, cutting mat, and quilt ruler
- Pins
- Sewing machine
- Fabric scissors
- Iron

WHOLE-CLOTH VERSION:

1. Enlarge and trace the Sunglasses Case pattern and cut it out with the paper scissors. Pin it to the exterior and lining fabrics and the batting (layered together or separately) and cut out one of each, using the rotary cutter, cutting mat, and quilt ruler.

2. Fuse the batting (following manufacturers' instructions) to the wrong side of the exterior fabric.

3. Layer the exterior and lining pieces, right sides together, and pin along the outer edges. Stitch the two pieces together using a ¼-in/6-mm seam allowance, and backstitching at the beginning and end to secure the seam, making sure to leave a 3-in-/7.5-cm-wide opening on the straight bottom edge for turning the case.

4. Clip the corners with the fabric scissors, and gently turn the case right-side out through the opening. Fold the opening edges under (to the wrong sides) ¼ in/ 6 mm, press with the iron, and pin it closed. Press the entire case flat, and topstitch only the top diagonal edge and bottom opening closed (see fig. 1).

5. Fold the sunglasses case in half vertically, pin the sides and bottom edges together, and topstitch all three sides to form the case, starting at the tall side of the diagonal opening, and sewing all the way around the perimeter to the top of the other side (see fig. 2).

Continued ➔

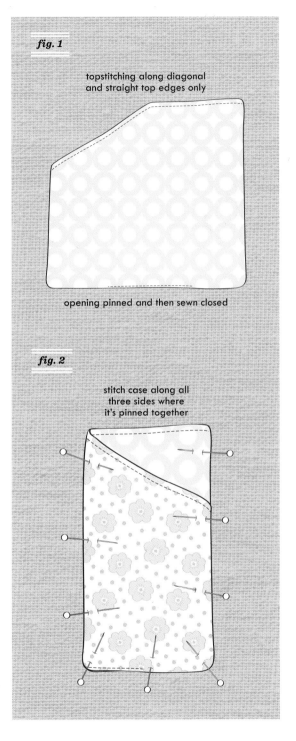

fig. 1

topstitching along diagonal and straight top edges only

opening pinned and then sewn closed

fig. 2

stitch case along all three sides where it's pinned together

PATCHWORK VERSION:

6. Arrange the four different 2½-by-9-in/6-by-23-cm strips of fabric horizontally so you like the mix. In that sequence, stitch the strips together along the long edges, using a ¼-in/6-mm seam allowance. Press the seams to one side, and topstitch along each seam.

7. Use this patchwork piece as your exterior fabric for the sunglasses case in step 1. You will have some extra room in the patchwork to maneuver, so feel free to align the pattern to catch pretty sections of fabric! Continue to follow the instructions for the whole-cloth version.

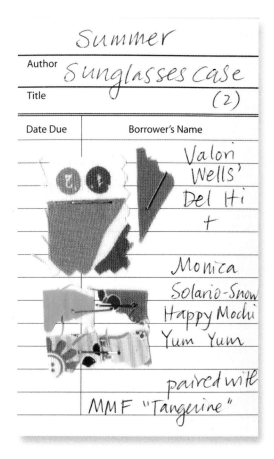

Date Due	Borrower's Name

Summer

Author Sunglasses Case

Title (2)

Valori
Wells'
Del Hi
+

Monica
Solario-Snow
Happy Mochi
Yum Yum

paired with
MMF "Tangerine"

PATCHWORK COASTERS & PLACEMATS

Stitch up an easy set of mix-and-match fabric coasters and placemats for your summer dining table. Coordinate bright and cheerful prints and solids in aqua, green, and white (or your favorite summer colors). The solid-fabric placemats are edged with a different contrasting print binding for an extra pop of pattern, while the coasters use the opposite arrangement—four print fabrics are used for the coaster tops, bordered by solids.

DIMENSIONS:

coasters: 4 in/10 cm square

placemats: 11 by 14 in/ 28 by 35.5 cm

TECHNIQUES USED:

Cutting without a pattern (page 14)

Stack and whack patchwork (page 25)

Seams (page 16)

Topstitching (page 16)

Folded finish binding (page 24)

Materials (for four coasters and four placemats):

¼ yd/0.25 m each of four different printed fabrics (44 in/112 cm wide), fabrics A, B, C, D, for tops

1 yd/1 m heavy double-sided fusible interfacing (22 in/56 cm wide) (I used fast2fuse)

Coordinating thread

½ yd/0.5 m each of coordinating solid fabrics (44 in/112 cm wide), fabrics 1, 2, 3, 4 (I used Michael Miller Cotton Couture in Limeade, Luna, Meadow, and Turquoise), for backing

Tools:

Rotary cutter, cutting mat, and quilt ruler

Digital camera (optional)

Sewing machine

Iron

1-in/2.5-cm binding tape maker

Continued →

COASTERS:

1. Using the rotary cutter, cutting mat, and quilt ruler, cut your fabrics and interfacing:

Fabric A, B, C, D: one 4-by-5½-in/10-by-14-cm rectangle of each print fabric (a total of four rectangles), for top

Fabric A, B, C, D: one 4-in/10-cm square of each print fabric (a total of four squares), for backing

Four 4-in/10-cm squares of heavy double-sided fusible interfacing

Fabric 1, 2, 3, 4: one 2-by-20-in/5-by-50-cm strip in each solid fabric (a total of four strips), for binding

2. Stack the 4-by-5½-in/10-by-14-cm rectangles, and diagonally cut them into four vertical sections (see fig. 1).

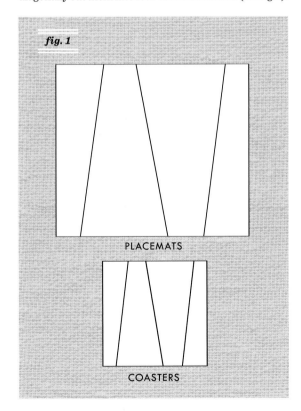

fig. 1

PLACEMATS

COASTERS

3. Mix and match the cut sections into four groups, arranging the pieces left to right, so each one is a different combination. Snap a photo with a digital camera for reference if you'd like to.

4. Piece the first coaster top from left to right, right sides together, stitching along the long edges with a ¼-in/6-mm seam allowance. Piece the other three coasters in the same way. Each pieced coaster top will be approximately 4 in/10 cm square after stitching.

5. Press each coaster top, back and front, pressing all seams the same direction. Topstitch along each seam. Using the iron, fuse one 4-in/10-cm square of backing fabric to one piece of double-sided interfacing, following the manufacturer's instructions. Turn the backing piece over, interface-side up, lay one pieced coaster top over it, right-side up, and fuse the pieced top to the interfacing. Trim any excess fabric from the sides so the three layers align along the edges.

6. Using the binding tape maker, make ½-in/12-mm double-folded binding tape from the four 2-in/5-cm strips of the four assorted solid fabrics. Starting with the bottom edge, bind one coaster with one of the solid fabrics, folding the binding at each of the four corners. Fold the final raw edge of binding under and stitch it down, covering the beginning edge of the binding tape.

7. Repeat steps 5 and 6, making three more coasters, binding each one with a different solid fabric.

Continued ➜

PLACEMATS:

8. Cut your fabrics and interfacing.

Fabric 1, 2, 3, 4: one 11-by-15½-in/28-by-39-cm rectangle of each solid fabric (a total of four rectangles) for tops

Fabric 1, 2, 3, 4: one 11-by-13½-in/28-by-34-cm rectangle of each solid fabric (a total of 4 rectangles) for backing

Four 11-by-13½-in/28-by-34-cm rectangles of heavy double-sided fusible interfacing

Fabric A, B, C, D: four 2-by-52-in/5-by-132-cm strips in each print fabric, for binding (strips can be joined together to get finished length)

9. Stack the assorted 11-by-15½-in/28-by-39-cm rectangles, and cut them diagonally into four vertical sections (see fig. 1, page 69).

10. Place these cut sections into four groups, arranging the pieces left to right so each group has a different color order combination. Snap a photo for reference if you'd like to.

11. Piece the first placemat top from left to right, right sides together, stitching each strip with a ¼-in/6-mm seam allowance. Piece the other three placemats in the same way. Each pieced placemat top will be an approximately 11-by-13½-in/28-by-34-cm rectangle after stitching.

12. Press each placemat top, back and front, pressing all seams the same direction. Topstitch along each seam. Using the iron, fuse one solid backing rectangle to one rectangle of double-sided fusible interfacing, following manufacturer's instructions. Turn the backing piece over, interface-side up, lay one pieced placemat top over it, right-side up, and fuse the top to the interfacing. Trim any excess fabric from the sides so the three layers align along the edges.

13. Make ½-in-/12-mm-wide double-folded binding tape from the 2-in/5-cm strips of the four assorted prints. Starting with the bottom edge, bind one placemat with one of the print fabrics, folding the binding at each of the four corners. Fold the final raw edge of binding under and stitch it down, covering the beginning of the binding tape (or you can carefully join it as you would a quilt or ring of binding if you prefer).

14. Repeat steps 12 and 13, making three more placemats, binding each one with a different print fabric.

BEACH TOTE BAG

I wanted to make a simple, sturdy tote bag for a day trip to the beach, just the right size to throw in a towel and swimsuit and go. So I came up with this easy-to-sew canvas tote and added a pair of outer pockets to spotlight a favorite piece of vintage Marimekko fabric. The pocket is the perfect size for tucking in a paperback or a magazine, keys, and sunscreen. Use matching or bright contrast binding along the pocket and bag openings to personalize your version!

DIMENSIONS:
14 in/36 cm tall

TECHNIQUES USED:
Cutting without a pattern (page 14)
Edge-stitching (page 17)
Seams (page 16)
Box corners (page 18)
Inserting a lining (page 19)
Binding (page 20)
Box-stitching (page 17)

Materials:

2/3 yd/0.6 m canvas, denim, or other heavy-weight or home dec fabric (60 in/152 cm wide) for the bag exterior (I used a pale green canvas)

1 yd/1 m solid quilting cotton fabric (44 in/112 cm wide) for lining and pocket binding (I used Michael Miller Cotton Couture in Meadow)

3/8 yd/0.4 m contrasting or print fabric (44 in/112 cm wide) for pocket and top opening binding (I used Marimekko Appelsiini)

3⅜ yd/3 m cotton webbing (1 in/2.5 cm wide) for handles

6-by-13-in/15-by-33-cm piece of plastic canvas (optional), for bottom insert

Coordinating thread

Tools:

Rotary cutter, cutting mat, and quilt ruler

Iron

Sewing machine

1-in/2.5-cm binding tape maker

Pins

Fabric marker

Continued →

1. Using the rotary cutter, cutting mat, and quilt ruler, cut your fabrics and trims.

EXTERIOR FABRIC:

> One 21-by-34-in/53-by-86-cm rectangle (on cross grain of fabric)

LINING FABRIC:

> One 21-by-34-in/53-by-86-cm rectangle, for interior

> One 10-by-24-in/25-by-61-cm rectangle, for pocket

> One 2-by-22-in/5-by-56-cm strip, for pocket binding

POCKET FABRIC:

> One 10-by-24-in/25-by-61-cm rectangle (on cross grain of fabric)

> One 2-by-42-in/5-by-107-cm strip, for top opening binding

WEBBING:

> One 120-in/305-cm piece, for handles

2. Prepare fabrics and trims. Press all fabric pieces with the iron. Join webbing into a continuous loop (making sure not to twist it), by overlapping the raw ends about ¼ to ⅜ in/6 mm to 1 cm and stitching overlap together with a tight zigzag stitch, using coordinating thread. Using the binding tape maker, make both of the 2-in-/5-cm-wide strips into ½-in-/12-mm-wide double-folded binding tape.

3. Align the pocket and pocket lining fabric rectangles, wrong sides together, and edge-stitch around the perimeter to join them. Pin the pocket binding over one short edge and stitch it down, then trim it flush with the edge. Repeat for the second short edge of the pocket. Press pocket piece, and with a fabric marker and quilt ruler, draw straight lines marking the centers of the long and short edges.

4. Lay out the exterior bag rectangle, right-side up, and again draw straight lines marking the center of the long and short edges. Set the pocket piece down, right-side up, on the exterior fabric, centering it by matching up

Continued →

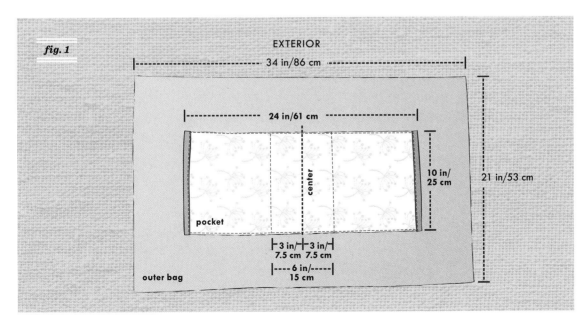

fig. 1

EXTERIOR

34 in/86 cm

24 in/61 cm

center

10 in/25 cm

21 in/53 cm

pocket

3 in/7.5 cm 3 in/7.5 cm

6 in/15 cm

outer bag

the center lines on both pieces. Pin the pocket in place along both long edges. Using the widthwise center line of the pocket as reference, draw two parallel lines 3 in/7.5 cm from the center line on either side (see fig. 1, page 73). Stitch through all layers, along both of these new parallel lines. Then edge-stitch both long edges of the pocket to the exterior. You have now defined the lower edge of each pocket and the bottom of the bag with the horizontal seams 6 in/15 cm apart.

5. Using the webbing join as a reference, mark the halfway point around the loop (approximately 60 in/152 cm from the join) with a pin. With the webbing lying flat, align the join and the pinned halfway point with the widthwise center line on the pocket and exterior (see fig. 2). Pin the webbing down over the sides of the pocket piece, making sure to cover the raw edges completely. Continue to pin the webbing all the way to the short edges of the exterior bag rectangle. Make sure the webbing handles line up with each other when you fold the bag in half. With a fabric marker, mark ¾ in/2 cm below the raw edges at the four places the webbing meets the exterior fabric.

6. Edge-stitch both sides of the handle in place, starting and stopping at each ¾-in/2-cm mark made in step 5. Repeat for the second handle side section.

7. Fold and pin the bag in half, aligning the short ends, right sides together, to form the sides of the bag. Stitch each side together with a ½-in/12-mm seam allowance, backstitching at the beginning and end of each seam.

8. Form a 3-in/7.5-cm box corner at the base of each side seam and stitch across each side of the base (see fig. 3). Don't cut the triangle off; instead fold and press it toward the center of the bag bottom on each side, and secure it with a short row of machine stitching. Turn exterior right-side out.

9. Fold the lining piece, right sides together, and repeat steps 7 and 8 to construct the lining in the same way as the outer bag. Instead of securing the box corners with stitching, you may trim them away. Keep the lining piece wrong-side out.

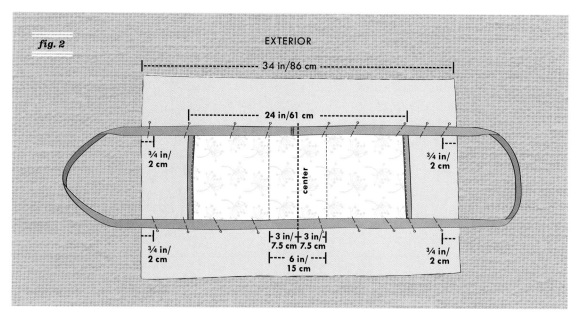

fig. 2

EXTERIOR

34 in/86 cm

24 in/61 cm

¾ in/2 cm

center

¾ in/2 cm

¾ in/2 cm

¾ in/2 cm

3 in/7.5 cm 3 in/7.5 cm

6 in/15 cm

10. If you want to reinforce the bottom of the bag, put a 6-by-13-in/15-by-33-cm piece of open-weave plastic canvas into it, trimming any excess away if need be. (This piece will provide stability but the bag will still be washable. Don't put anything with plastic canvas in it into the dryer, though.)

11. Insert the lining into the exterior, wrong sides together, aligning the side seams. Pin around the top perimeter of the bag and edge-stitch to join the two layers, being careful to avoid sewing the handles (fold them down and away from where you are stitching).

12. Measure the bag's opening (mine measured 40 in/ 102 cm), and trim the remaining piece of binding to 1/2 in/12 mm longer than the opening. Form a binding ring with a 1/4-in/6-mm join and pin it over the raw edges of the bag opening, avoiding catching the handles in your stitching by folding them down and away from the top of the bag.

13. Stitch the binding around the top perimeter of the bag.

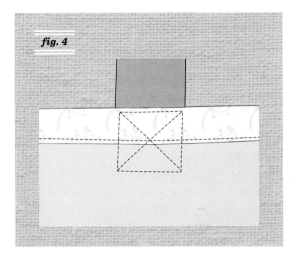

fig. 4

14. Pin each of the four handle ends in place over the binding to secure. Sew a box stitch at each of the four handle-bag intersections, to securely join them, stitching through all layers (see fig. 4).

15. With a little water, remove any visible marks from the fabric marker. Fill your bag with everything you need to head to the beach!

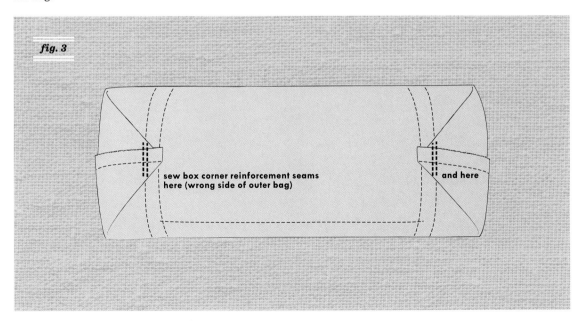

fig. 3

sew box corner reinforcement seams here (wrong side of outer bag)   and here

PICNIC QUILT

A bright, cheerful quilt spread out in a park or your backyard is the essence of summer to me—having a picnic is such a nice way to spend a long, sunny afternoon. I chose four of my favorite summer colors and found a dozen pretty prints to mix into the picnic quilt of my dreams.

After piecing a few dozen string blocks one by one, I hosted a little quilting bee at my house one summer day. Four of my Portland Modern Quilt Guild friends came over to piece quilt blocks with me…and, a couple of hours later, thanks to the generosity of friends, I had sixty-four string quilt blocks ready to arrange into a colorful series of bold diamonds and happy supporting fabrics. When I finished my quilt top, another PMQG friend, Nancy Stovall, professionally quilted it for me in a pattern of flowers and leaves—a beautiful finishing touch!

Since so many people stitched blocks for this quilt, we ended up with slightly wonky blocks (as you can see in the overall design). I love this slightly off-kilter diamond design, but you can match your diagonal "strings" with perfect precision if you prefer.

In the directions, I describe one 8-in/20-cm string block as a block, and four of the joined blocks as a diamond (since the four center strips form a bold, eye-catching diamond shape when they're united). You'll have a chance to combine your sixteen diamonds into a unique overall pattern—each stage of making the quilt is a new opportunity to pair colors and fabrics! Your quilt will measure 60 in/152 cm square, with this size and number of blocks.

DIMENSIONS:
60 in/152 cm square

TECHNIQUES USED:
Cutting without a pattern (page 14)
String quilting (page 26)
Seams (page 16)
Quilting (page 27)
Edge-stitching (page 17)
Binding (page 20)

Continued →

NOTE:

You can stitch and arrange your string blocks however you like for a lovely effect. If you want to make a quilt like this one, you'll start each block with a 2-in-/5-cm-wide strip of solid fabric—sixteen each of four fabrics of different colors. Then build the blocks with any print fabrics, as well as mixing in the same solids here and there. If you have less than 1/3 yd/0.3 m of a few print fabrics, just use what you have of those, perhaps supplementing with more of other prints. You may end up with leftover strips of some fabrics, which will be perfect to use later for small patchwork projects.

Materials:

3 yd/2.75 m muslin (44 in/112 cm wide) or 1½ yd/1.5 m muslin (90 in/229 cm wide), for foundation blocks

½ yd/0.5 m each four different solid fabrics (44 in/112 cm wide) for quilt top (I used Michael Miller's Cotton Couture in Sun, Coral, Tangerine, and Bright White)

1/3 yd/0.3 m each of twelve assorted print fabrics (44 in/112 cm wide) in complementary colors, for quilt top

3¾ yd/3.5 m fabric (44 in/112 cm wide) for pieced backing, or a vintage sheet or other fabric for backing, at least 66 in/168 cm square (I used a vintage Vera flat sheet, full size, trimmed to target the floral pattern)

64-in/163-cm square piece of batting

½ yd/0.5 m fabric (44 in/112 cm wide), for binding (I used Michael Miller's Cotton Couture in Sun)

Coordinating thread

Tools:

Rotary cutter, cutting mat, and quilt ruler

8-in/20-cm square template quilt ruler (recommended)

Iron

Sewing machine

Digital camera

Pencil and paper or Post-it notes

Pins

Curved safety pins

1-in/2.5-cm binding tape maker

1. Prepare the muslin foundation blocks: Using the rotary cutter, cutting mat, and quilt ruler or square template ruler, cut 8-in-/20-cm-wide strips of the muslin across the fabric, selvage to selvage (or make a small cut at one side and tear the muslin for a quicker approach). Then use the 8-in/20-cm square quilt ruler to trim the long strips into a total of sixty-four blocks. In this step and steps 2 and 3, remember to trim off the selvages, so they don't accidentally get sewn into your blocks. Press each block with the iron and set aside in a stack.

2. Cut a total of six 2-in-/5-cm-wide strips of each of the solid fabrics, selvage to selvage, for the block centers. You'll need to make sixteen of each color, and you will have some shorter strips left over to mix in with your prints as you go. Also cut a few narrower strips of solids to mix in. (I cut one 1-in/2.5-cm and one 1½-in-/4-cm-wide strip of each of my solids.)

3. Cut the twelve print fabrics into strips of varying widths. (I cut each of my prints into six to eight strips, selvage to selvage, each one measuring 1 in/2.5 cm, 1½ in/4 cm, 2 in/5 cm, or 2½ in/6 cm wide. See Note. You may need to cut a few extra strips of various prints at the end to make sure you maintain a nice combination of colors, and everyone pieces differently, but this number is a good ballpark estimate for what you'll need to make a string quilt this size. I mixed my strings up on my sewing table so I could just reach for a new fabric each time without thinking about it too much, and added the solid strip ends into the pile when they were too short for block centers. I didn't follow a pattern or segregate colors; I just tried to get a nice mix of color and pattern in each block.)

4. Following the general directions for string quilting, start each block by pinning a 2-in/5-cm solid strip diagonally across the center of a muslin square right-side up (see fig. 28B, String quilting, page 27). (You should get three center strips out of each solid strip, with some left over at the end that you can mix into your blocks.) Lay a second strip of printed fabric over it, right sides together, aligned along the right edge. Stitch through all layers with a ¼-in/6-mm seam allowance. Press and trim down both strips.

5. Continue adding more fabric strips to the left and right, pressing and trimming as you go, until the muslin square is completely full of diagonally pieced fabrics.

6. Flip the block over and trim all excess fabric strips neatly to 8-in/20-cm square, using a square template (or quilt ruler) and rotary cutter (see fig. 28F, String quilting, page 27). Press again.

7. Working in this way, create sixteen blocks, using each of your four solid colors as the center, for a total of sixty-four 8-in/20-cm blocks. Sort them by the color of the center stripe.

8. Arrange the sixteen blocks in your first color into four 4-block diamonds, so you like the fabric arrangements and mix (see fig. 1). Take a digital photo and look at that, too.

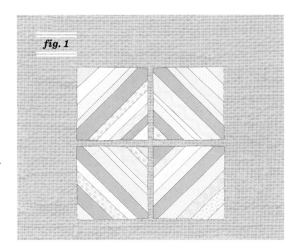

fig. 1

9. When you're happy with the arrangement of your four diamonds, bring the first one to your sewing table. Stitch the two top blocks, right sides together, with a ¼-in/6-mm seam allowance. Then stitch the two bottom blocks together the same way.

10. Align the two joined blocks, matching and pinning the center seams, and stitch them right sides together with a ¼-in/6-mm seam allowance. Press seams to one side, then press back and front, and set them aside. This is your first diamond.

11. Repeat, joining the remaining blocks in this color into three more diamonds.

12. Make sets of four diamonds in each of the other colors the same way, so you have a total of sixteen 4-block diamonds.

Continued ➔

13. Arrange your diamonds in four rows of four, mixing colors so you like the effect. (I followed a simple rule of not repeating a color in a row or column, so they were fairly randomized. In my diamonds, the white reads much more clearly than the yellow, coral, or orange, so I made sure to scatter my white diamonds farther apart from each other on the grid, so the quilt had good color movement.)

14. Take a photo of your diamonds arrangement and look at it on screen. You may want to do some rearranging after seeing the tones in a photograph.

15. When you are happy with the final arrangement, take a photo for reference. With pencil and paper or Post-it notes, label the first (leftmost) diamond of each horizontal row 1, 2, 3, and 4, and pin or stick the numbers to the diamond. Stack each row, from left to right, with the first, labeled diamond on the top of each.

16. With the stack of diamonds for the first row, pin the first and second diamonds, right sides together, matching center seams. Stitch them together with a ¼-in/6-mm seam allowance. Working left to right, stitch the third diamond to the second, then the fourth to the third. Press seams to one side, then press this row back and front.

17. Repeat to sew the second, third, and fourth rows, pressing each one as you finish.

18. Pin the first horizontal row to the second one, right sides together, matching all seven vertical seams, and stitch them with a ¼-in/6-mm seam allowance.

19. Repeat, sewing the third and fourth rows to finish your quilt top.

20. Make the quilt sandwich. Place the backing fabric on the floor, right-side down. Place the batting over it. Then place the quilt top over both layers, right-side up. Use curved safety pins to hold the layers together.

21. Quilt your picnic quilt as desired. Using straight lines for quilting is the most beginner-friendly pattern, while free-motion quilting (creating designs that move around the quilt) and other more elaborate patterns are wonderful, too. (I commissioned my friend Nancy Stovall to finish my quilt on her long-arm machine.)

22. Edge-stitch around the perimeter of the quilt and then trim away the excess batting and backing fabric with a rotary cutter and quilt ruler, moving a cutting mat underneath as you work your way around the quilt.

23. Cut six 2-in-/5-cm-wide strips of the binding fabric and join them; then, using the binding tape maker, make ½-in/12-mm double-folded binding tape. Starting with the bottom edge, bind your quilt, folding each of the four corners, and finishing with a join.

fall

Author

Title French press + coffee
cup cozy set

Date Due

Borrower's Name

pearl bracelet,
Heath crosshatch,
botanical prints

Products, Inc.

COZY WOOL SCARF

Inspired by the colors of fall leaves, this soft wool scarf has a special touch: It's lined with silk for a light and luxurious finish. I paired a tonal plaid merino with burnt-orange silk, but you can make it in the colors or patterns you like best. It's also very easy to sew, as long as you temper the slipperiness of the silk with a quick hand-basting first. Wear it to celebrate the first crisp days of autumn!

DIMENSIONS:
6½ by 60 in/16.5 by 152 cm

TECHNIQUES USED:
Cutting without a pattern (page 14)
Hand-basting (page 15)
Turning right-side out (page 17)
Edge-stitching (page 17)

NOTE:

You can join two shorter pieces of wool or silk together with a ½-in/12-mm seam allowance to obtain the 7-by-62-in/17-by-158-cm pieces to start with (or simply make your scarf narrower or shorter). When joining two pieces of silk, I suggest following the same hand-basting directions given to sew silk and wool together. A Microtex (sharp) machine needle is ideal for this project.

Materials:

7-by-62-in/17-by-158-cm piece of lining-weight silk

7-by-62-in/17-by-158-cm piece of soft wool in a complementary color

Contrasting thread, for basting

Coordinating thread

Tools:

Iron

Pins

Hand-sewing needle

Microtex sewing machine needle

Sewing machine

Seam ripper

Fabric scissors

Chopstick

Continued →

1. Carefully press the silk fabric with a low-heat iron and no steam under a protective pressing cloth. Carefully press the wool fabric, after adjusting your iron temperature setting to "wool," and steam, again using a pressing cloth.

2. Pin the long rectangle of silk to the wool fabric around all four sides, right sides together. Using a needle and thread in a contrasting color, hand-baste the fabrics together along all four sides with long running stitches (I like to use a backstitch every five or six stitches to hold the seam), ¼ in/6 mm from the edge. Don't bother to knot your basting stitches: You'll want to be able to remove them easily after you machine-sew. Leave a 5-in/12-cm opening unbasted along one long side for turning right-side out later.

3. Starting at one end of the unbasted section, and using the Microtex (sharp) needle, machine-stitch all four sides of the silk and wool fabrics together, with a ¼-in/6-mm seam allowance. Stop at the other end of the 5-in/12-cm opening. Be sure to backstitch at the beginning and end of the seam.

4. Remove all your hand-basting stitches with a seam ripper or scissors. Clip the corners and turn the scarf and lining right-sides out, gently pushing out the corners with a chopstick.

5. Press your scarf using a pressing cloth (on low/medium setting) and carefully fold the raw edges of the opening under ¼ in/6 mm. Pin the opening together. Edge-stitch around the perimeter of the scarf, including the opening, backstitching at the beginning and end of the seam to secure.

PATCHWORK POTHOLDERS & TRIVET

The kitchen is such a nice place to be in the cooler months of autumn, and I wanted to make a set of potholders and a trivet in warm colors for cooking and baking. (Believe it or not, this autumn-colors project uses the same string-piecing technique of the summery picnic quilt, just a few pages earlier.) Scrap-friendly string piecing means this entire three-piece patchwork project uses only seven strips of fabric (backed with remnants) to create the whole set.

DIMENSIONS:

Potholders: 7 in/17 cm square
Trivet: 9 in/23 cm square

TECHNIQUES USED:

Cutting without a pattern (page 14)
String quilting (page 26)
Seams (page 16)
Quilting (page 27)
Edge-stitching (page 17)
Binding (page 20)

Materials (for two potholders and one trivet):

7 strips of print and solid fabrics of your choice (44 in/112 cm wide), cut selvage to selvage (I cut two strips 1½ in/4 cm wide, three strips 2 in/5 cm wide, and two strips 2½ in/6 cm wide for this set), for patchwork tops

Two 7-in/17-cm squares and one 9-in/23-cm square of muslin, for quilting foundation

Coordinating thread

Two 7-in/17-cm squares and one 9-in/23-cm square of Insul-Bright thermal batting

Two 7-in/17-cm squares and one 9-in/23-cm square of low-loft batting

Two 7½-in/19-cm squares and one 9½-in/24-cm square of any print or solid fabric, for backing

¼ yd/.25 m fabric in print of your choice to be cut into 2-in-/5-cm-strips, for binding tape, for the three items (35 in/89 cm for each potholder, 38 in/97 cm for the trivet), pressed into a total of 108 in/274 cm of ½-in/12-mm double-folded binding tape

Continued →

Harvest Soup

- carrots
- onions
- squash
- potatoes
- garlic

Tools:

  Rotary cutter, cutting mat, and quilt ruler

  Iron

  Pins

  Sewing machine

  1-in/2.5-cm binding tape maker

POTHOLDERS AND TRIVET

1. Using the rotary cutter, cutting mat, and quilt ruler, cut all fabrics to the given measurements, and press all fabric pieces with the iron.

POTHOLDER (MAKES TWO):

2. Following the general directions for string quilting, choose a center fabric strip and place it diagonally across the center of a muslin square (see fig. 28B, String quilting, page 27). Pin it in place. Lay a second strip over it, right sides together, aligned along the right edge. Stitch through all layers with a ¼-in/6-mm seam allowance. Press and trim down both strips.

3. Continue adding more fabric strips to the left and right, pressing and trimming as you go, until the muslin square is completely full of diagonally pieced fabrics.

4. Flip the block over and trim all excess fabric strips neatly to a 7-in/17-cm square, using a quilt ruler and rotary cutter (see fig. 28F, String quilting, page 27). Press again.

5. Repeat steps 2–4 to make a second string block the same way, using the fabric strips in different colored and patterned combinations.

6. Layer each 7-in/17-cm patchwork square over one square each of Insul-Bright batting and low-loft batting, then the 7½-in/19-cm backing fabric, to make small quilt sandwiches. Pin the layers together.

7. Quilt as desired (I quilted mine in horizontal lines 1 in/2.5 cm apart with olive-green thread). Then edge-stitch around the perimeter of each quilted square, and trim any excess fabric or batting to neatly square up the 7-in/17-cm potholders.

8. Using the binding tape maker, make two 35 in/89 cm strips of double-folded binding tape. Machine-bind each potholder, starting at the upper right-hand corner of the design. Fold the binding at the corners and continue around the potholder clockwise. When you reach the original starting point, cut a 5-in/12-cm tail of extra binding extending off the square and continue stitching to the end. Then fold the tail into a loop to the back of the potholder, folding the raw edge under and stitching it down securely.

TRIVET:

9. Make the trivet the same way as you did the potholders, but as a 9-in/23-cm square. Also, you won't make a binding loop, but instead, start and finish binding on the bottom edge of the trivet and carefully join the binding tape's edges as you would when binding a quilt (or you can fold the final raw edge of binding under and stitch it down, covering the beginning of the binding tape, for a simpler finish).

SKETCHBOOK COVER

This simple fabric cover with side flaps slips over any plain notebook or journal to make your craft sketchbook a bit prettier! The cover is a perfect back-to-school project as well. You can make a one-fabric cover using an interesting print, or pair two fabrics in a patchwork version. I used a Moleskine sketchbook and added a bookmark made of measuring tape–printed twill tape to mine, too.

DIMENSIONS: variable

TECHNIQUES USED:

Cutting without a pattern (page 14)

Seams (page 16)

Turning right-side out (page 17)

Binding (page 20)

Edge-stitching (page 17)

Rule of thirds patchwork (for patchwork version) (see Note, page 50)

Topstitching (page 16)

Materials:

Blank notebook or journal

Exterior fabric(s) of your choice (see step 1 to estimate quantity)

Lining fabric (see step 1 to estimate quantity)

Coordinating thread

2-in/5-cm strip of fabric for binding (can be lining, exterior, or a contrasting fabric)

Twill tape (⅜ in/1 cm wide), for bookmark (see step 6 to estimate length) (optional)

Tools:

Measuring tape

Rotary cutter, cutting mat, and quilt ruler

Pins

Sewing machine

Iron

1-in/2.5-cm binding tape maker

Seam ripper (optional)

Continued →

ONE-FABRIC COVER VERSION:

Width of your book (lying flat): _____
+ 6 in/15 cm

= **WIDTH OF COVER PATTERN** _____

Height of book: _____
+ 1 in/2.5 cm

= **HEIGHT OF COVER PATTERN** _____

Height of book: _____
+ 2 in/5 cm

= **BOOKMARK LENGTH:** _____

1. With a measuring tape, measure the height and width of your notebook when it is closed and when it is open with the pages pressed flat (see fig. 1). (My 120-page Moleskine sketchbook was 10 by 7 ½ in/ 25 by 19 cm, when closed, and 10 by 15 in/25 by 38 cm when open lying flat.) Add 1 in/2.5 cm to the height

and 6 in/15 cm to the width of your open-book mea- surement for your cover pattern size (mine was 11 by 21 in/28 by 53 cm, see fig. 1).

2. Using the rotary cutter, cutting mat, and quilt ruler, cut a piece of exterior fabric and a piece of lining fabric to the cover pattern size (in my example, 11 by 21 in/28 by 53 cm). Pin the two pieces right sides together, along the top and bottom long edges only. Then stitch the pinned edges together with a ¼-in/ 6-mm seam allowance.

3. Turn the lined cover right-side out through one of the short ends and press with the iron. Trim the raw edges on the two open sides so they're neat and straight.

4. Using the binding tape maker, make a piece of dou- ble-folded binding tape with your choice of lining, exterior, or another contrasting fabric, to cover the two side raw edges (the flaps) of your book cover. Mea- sure the cover's height (for my cover, 10½ in/26.5 cm) and add 1 in/2.5 cm (making it 11½ in/29 cm) to each side (so 23 in/58 cm total). Pin a piece of binding tape

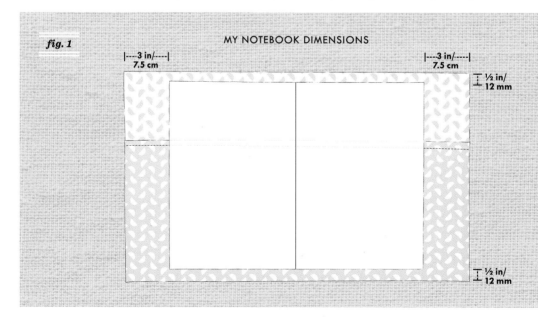

fig. 1   MY NOTEBOOK DIMENSIONS

|----3 in/----|
7.5 cm

|----3 in/----|
7.5 cm

½ in/
12 mm

½ in/
12 mm

over each of the two raw edges, centering it, and stitch it down. Trim each binding tape edge to extend ½ in/ 12 mm beyond the top and bottom edges of the cover.

5. Place your notebook on the cover (lining-side up) and fold and pin the flaps in place (see fig. 2). Close the notebook to make sure the cover lies smoothly. Now make sure your flaps are even (about 3 in/7.5 cm wide) and tuck the raw edges of the binding tape inside the flap fold.

6. To add an optional bookmark, add 2 in/5 cm to your cover's height and cut a piece of twill tape to that length. Measure about ½ in/12 mm to the right from the center of the cover (a little farther over, like 1 in/2.5 cm, for a thicker notebook), and gently open a few stitches at the top of the cover with a seam ripper. Tuck one raw-edge end of twill tape or ribbon inside, about ½ in/12 mm, and pin to secure it. Trim the other end at an angle to minimize fraying.

7. Take the notebook out, keeping the flaps pinned in place, and press all along the top and bottom edges.

Edge-stitch along the top edge, backstitching at beginning and end of the seam to secure, and stitching the small bookmark opening closed. Repeat at the bottom edge.

PATCHWORK COVER VERSION:

8. Follow step 1 to find your cover pattern size (in my case, 11 by 21 in/28 by 53 cm). I used a simple version of stacking two contrasting fabrics together vertically, using the general rule of thirds (but you can do any kind of patchwork design you like). Using your cover pattern measurements, cut two fabrics (a smaller one, 4¼ by 21 in/11 by 53 cm, for the top section, and a larger one, 7¼ by 21 in/18 by 53 cm, for the bottom section), adding ¼ in/6 mm to each section for seam allowance. Stitch them together with a ¼-in/6-mm seam allowance to create an exterior piece that is 11 by 21 in/28 by 53 cm. Press the seam to one side and top-stitch it, then continue sewing the cover as instructed in step 2.

10. Finish the cover as instructed in steps 3–7 for the one-fabric cover version.

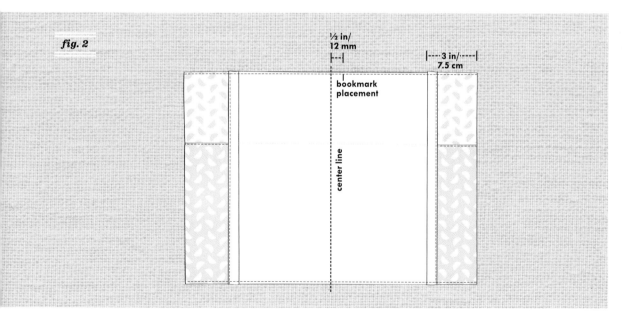

fig. 2

½ in/
12 mm

3 in/
7.5 cm

bookmark
placement

center line

FRENCH PRESS & COFFEE CUP COZIES

I love coffee and I'm rarely without it in the mornings. I needed cozies for my French press coffee maker and my favorite to-go coffee cup, so I decided to sew them in a mix of pretty prints. I chose deep, dark, coffee brown so the inevitable sloshes and spills don't show!

DIMENSIONS:

coffee cup cozy: 3 by $10\frac{1}{2}$ in/7.5 by 26.5 cm

French press cozy: $6\frac{1}{2}$ by 11 in/16.5 by 28 cm

TECHNIQUES USED:

Cutting without a pattern (page 14)

Cutting with a pattern (page 14)

Seams (page 16)

Turning right-side out (page 17)

Topstitching (page 16)

Stitching a loop (see step 13)

Edge-stitching (page 17)

Sewing on a button (page 20)

PATTERN NEEDED:

Coffee Cup Cozy pattern (see page 138)

Continued →

Materials (for both cozies):

⅛ yd/12 cm of each of four print fabrics of your choice (or you can use remnants), fabrics A, B, C, D, for exterior

¼ yd/0.25 m coordinating solid fabric (I used Michael Miller Cotton Couture in Chocolate), for lining and exterior

¼ yd/0.25 m fusible batting

1½-in/4-cm piece of sew-in Velcro

9-in/23-cm piece (⅛ in/3 mm wide) narrow elastic

Two ⅞-in/2.25-cm buttons (or the size of your choice)

Tools:

Quilt ruler and pencil

Paper scissors

Pattern paper

Rotary cutter and cutting mat

Sewing machine

Iron

Fabric scissors

Pins

Seam ripper

Hand-sewing needle

CUP COZY:

1. Using the quilt ruler and pencil, create a paper pattern that is a 2½-by-4-in/6-by-10-cm rectangle, and cut it out with the paper scissors. Ideally use pattern paper that is semi-opaque, so you can capture any part of the fabric print you like. Enlarge the Coffee Cup Cozy pattern and trace it onto pattern paper, transferring marks. Cut out the pattern.

2. Using your rectangle pattern from step 1, rotary cutter, cutting mat, and quilt ruler, cut one each of the four print fabrics. Also cut three 1½-by-4-in/4-by-10-cm strips of the solid lining fabric.

3. Arrange the rectangles in a row so you like the mix of fabric prints left to right: we'll call them A, B, C, D. With right sides together, stitch A to a strip of the solid lining fabric along a 4-in/10-cm side with a ¼-in/6-mm seam allowance, then stitch B to the other long edge of the solid fabric the same way. Sew another strip of solid fabric to the other side of B, then add C, a strip of solid fabric, and finally D. Your four prints will be in order, neatly separated by thin strips of your solid lining fabric (see fig. 1 for an example of this arrangement).

4. Press your finished patchwork panel front and back with the iron, pressing the seams toward the solid panels each time. Following package instructions, fuse the batting to the wrong side of the panel. Topstitch along each edge of your solid fabric strips.

5. Pin the Coffee Cup Cozy pattern over the patchwork-batting panel and cut it out (see fig. 1) with the fabric scissors, and then cut a second cozy shape out of your solid lining fabric. Layer and pin the patchwork-batting piece and lining piece, right sides together, and stitch around the perimeter using a ¼-in/6-mm seam allowance, leaving a 2½-in/6-cm opening on the bottom edge. Backstitch at the beginning and end of the seam to secure.

6. Clip the corners and turn right-side out. Press raw edges under at the opening, pinning it closed, and press all edges flat. Edge-stitch around the perimeter of the cozy, including the opening, backstitching at the beginning and end of the seam to secure it.

7. Wrap the cozy around your coffee cup and mark where the overlap is. Separate your Velcro into pieces and edge-stitch one piece on the outside left edge, and the other piece to the inside right edge, so they line up for closing when the cozy is on the cup.

FRENCH PRESS COZY

8. Using the same rectangle pattern you created to make the coffee cup cozy, cut two rectangles of each of the four print fabrics for a total of eight rectangles, capturing any print pattern you'd like. Cut three 1½-by-7½-in/4-by-19-cm strips of the solid lining fabric.

9. Arrange your rectangles in a row so you like the mix of patterns left to right: we'll call them A, B, C, and D. Pair them with a second set of contrasting rectangles below, like a double-decker version of the coffee cup

cozy (see fig. 2). With right sides together, stitch each of the vertical pairs with a ¼-in/6-mm seam allowance. You can use any combination you like. Press the seams to one side.

10. With right sides together, stitch your first vertical pair of print rectangles to a strip of the solid lining fabric, along a 7½-in/19-cm side, using a ¼-in/6-mm seam allowance. Then join the second vertical pair of print rectangles to the other long edge of the solid fabric in the same way. Sew another strip of solid fabric to the other side of the second pair, then add the third vertical pair, a strip of solid fabric, and finally

Continued ➔

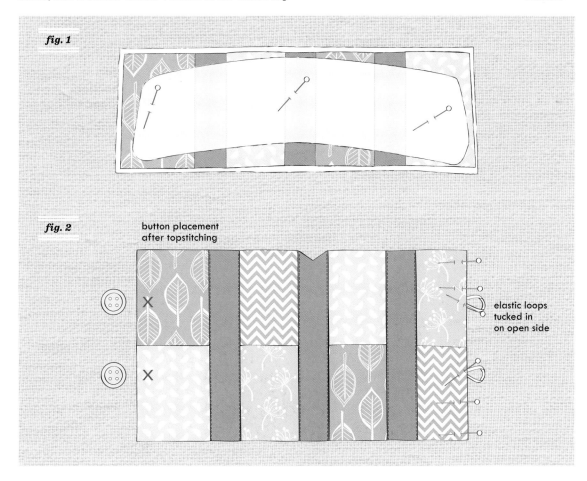

fig. 1

fig. 2

button placement after topstitching

elastic loops tucked in on open side

the fourth pair. The four sets of prints will be in order, neatly separated by thin strips of the solid fabric.

11. Press your finished patchwork panel front and back, pressing the seams toward the solid panels each time. Following the package instructions, fuse the batting to the wrong side of the panel. Topstitch along each edge of your solid fabric strips.

12. Cut a piece of solid lining fabric the same size as your patchwork panel (7½ by 11½ in/19 by 29 cm) and pin them right sides together. Mark the top center with a pin or fabric marker, and cut a neat ⅜-in/1-cm *V* at the mark out of both layers for the French press spout. Leaving one short side open, stitch around the perimeter with a ¼-in/6-mm seam allowance.

13. Trim the corners and gently turn the French press cozy right-side out, smoothing the *V.* Press the raw edges to the inside ¼ in/6 mm along the unsewn short side. Wrap the cozy around your French press and mark where the inner section of the handle is with pins (see fig. 2, page 97). Cut two 4½-in/11-cm pieces of the elastic and fold them into loops, pinning them into the folded, unsewn edge of the cozy, inside those handle markings. (Mine measured 2 in/5 cm from the top edge and 3 in/7.5 cm from the bottom edge, but fit your cozy to your French press so it works well with your handle.)

14. Edge-stitch around the entire perimeter of the French press cozy, following the line of the *V* and stitching down the pinned section to catch the raw ends of the elastic loops securely.

15. Hand-sew two buttons to the other side of the cozy with needle and thread, matching the position of the elastic loops.

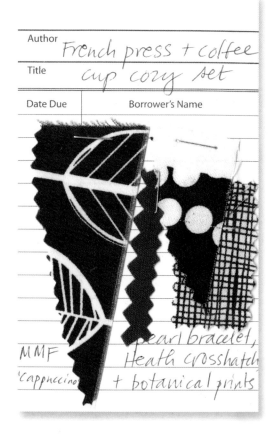

Author *French press + coffee*
Title *cup cozy set*

Date Due | Borrower's Name

MMF
Cappuccino

pearl bracelet,
Heath crosshatch
+ botanical prints

PATCHWORK THROW

This cozy patchwork quilt, made up of a beautiful mix of Pendleton wools, is an autumn favorite of mine. I originally sewed one the week before my little boy, Everett, was born, and cuddling him all wrapped up in it was so nice and comforting. It's perfect for snuggling while watching a movie at home, or sitting outside on a chilly night. Mix any weights or styles of wool fabric you like for the patchwork, though using a majority of medium-weight fabrics (like old blankets or new yardage) instead of all shirt-weight wools makes for a nice sturdy throw.

DIMENSIONS:
68 by 48 in/173 by 122 cm

TECHNIQUES USED:
Cutting with a pattern (optional) (page 14)
Cutting without a pattern (page 14)
Seams (page 16)
Turning right-side out (page 17)
Edge-stitching (page 17)

Materials:

Assorted wool fabrics: enough to cut forty-nine 7-by-10-in/17-by-25-cm rectangles. Depending on fabric widths, about ⅓ yd/0.3 m of each will work. I used nine different fabrics and cut between one and seven squares of each one, so feel free to mix in remnants and just cut fewer squares of those fabrics you have smaller quantities of.

Coordinating thread

2 yd/2 m solid-color wool fabric (60 in/152 cm wide), for plain backing (an old blanket is perfect for this)

Tools:

Pattern paper and pencil

Paper scissors (optional)

Fabric scissors

Rotary cutter, cutting mat, and quilt ruler

Digital camera

Paper or Post-it notes

Pins

Sewing machine

Iron

Continued →

1. Create a rectangle pattern with pattern paper, pencil, quilt ruler, and scissors or simply cut your wool fabrics with a rotary cutter, cutting mat, and quilt ruler into a total of forty-nine 7-by-10-in/17-by-25-cm rectangles for your patchwork quilt top. You can use any number of fabrics you like, but including seven or more gives you the most design flexibility.

2. Using a large table or floor as a work surface, arrange the forty-nine wool rectangles in rows, seven across and seven down. Arrange and rearrange until you have a nice mix of color and value. I arranged my rectangles so there were no repeats in a row (horizontal) or column (vertical) to randomize the mix, but you can organize yours however you like. When you are working on the overall design, I recommend taking a photo now and then and looking at that along the way. You may want to do some rearranging after seeing the tones in the photo.

3. When you are happy with the final arrangement, take a digital photo for reference. With a pencil and paper or Post-it notes, label the first (leftmost) rectangle of each horizontal row 1–7 and pin or stick the numbers to the rectangles.

4. Stack the first row of rectangles, working left to right, with the labeled (1) rectangle on top.

5. With right sides together, stitch the first rectangle to the second one using a ⅜-in/1-cm seam allowance (along the short 7-in/17-cm sides). Then stitch the second to the third, and so on, until you have sewn your first row of seven rectangles. Press the seams to one side with the iron, then press the front and back, and replace the row on the floor or table.

6. Repeat steps 4 and 5 to assemble the next six rows of seven rectangles.

7. With right sides together, pin the bottom edge of row 1 to the top edge of row 2, matching all vertical seams, and stitch together with a ⅜-in/1-cm seam allowance. Press the joining seam to one side.

8. Repeat step 7 to continue adding rows 3–7 to the patchwork design, pressing each seam as you go. This is your patchwork top!

9. To add a plain back, measure your patchwork top and cut a piece of solid wool the same size.

10. Place the solid back on the floor or table, right-side up, and place the patchwork top over it, right-side down. Align them together and pin around the perimeter, leaving two squares (about 20 in/50 cm) of the bottom edge unpinned as an opening for turning.

11. Stitch around the perimeter of the throw with a ⅜-in/1-cm seam allowance, leaving the opening unsewn.

12. Clip the corners and turn the patchwork throw right-side out through the opening. Fold and press the raw edges of the opening under ⅜ in/1 cm and pin them in place. Edge-stitch around the entire perimeter of the throw, including the pinned opening, backstitching at the beginning and end of the seam to secure it.

13. Press your patchwork throw, front and back.

WINTER

HOLIDAY GARLAND

Handmade holiday decorations are one of my favorite things to make, and I always enjoy mixing fabrics in my projects. This super-simple garland of circles uses lots of the same prints I use for the Mason Jar & Wine Bottle Cozies (page 115) and the Holiday Ornaments (page 107); the garland is perfect for scraps since you need so little of each fabric. You can use twelve different fabrics and reverse each circle to an alternate print, as I did, or keep the design more streamlined with fewer prints.

DIMENSIONS:
72 in/183 cm long

TECHNIQUES USED:
Tracing a pattern (page 14)
End loop (see steps 5 and 6)
Sewing on a button
(page 20)

PATTERN USED:
Holiday Garland pattern
(page 139)

NOTE:

You can use an automatic cutter like an AccuQuilt Go! cutter to cut your 2-in/5-cm circles in Step 2 if you prefer, but you may want to start with larger pieces of fabric (say 6 by 12 in/15 by 30.5 cm) so you have enough space at the edges.

Materials (for a 6-ft/2-m garland):
5-by-8-in/12-by-20-cm piece each of twelve assorted printed fabrics (I used red, light blue, gray, and white), for garland circles

Three 9-by-12-in/23-by-30.5-cm sheets of Steam-A-Seam or other lightweight double-sided fusible web

Coordinating thread

6-in/15-cm piece of rickrack or ribbon, for hanging loops

4 small buttons, up to $3/4$ in/2 cm across

Tools:
Iron

Fabric scissors

Pattern paper and pencil

Paper scissors

Pins

AccuQuilt Go! cutter (optional)

Digital camera (optional)

Sewing machine

Hand-sewing needle

Continued →

1. Press each 5-by-8-in/12-by-20-cm piece of printed fabric with the iron, and pair the twelve rectangles into six combinations you like together. Cut the three pieces of double-sided fusible web in half with fabric scissors, yielding six pieces, and trim each of them to 5 by 8 in/12 by 20 cm. Following manufacturer's instructions, fuse each of the fabric pairs, wrong sides together, with the double-sided fusible web between them so you have six double-sided pieces of fabric.

2. Trace the Holiday Garland pattern with pattern paper and pencil. Cut it out with paper scissors, and pin it to the upper corner of your first piece of double-sided fabric. Cut out the 2-in/5-cm garland circle and set it aside. Continue to cut out five more 2-in/5-cm circles the same way. You'll cut a total of thirty-six circles, six from each of the six double-sided fabric rectangles. Alternatively, you can use an AccuQuilt Go! cutter to cut your fabrics.

3. Lay the circles out in a long row, mixing your fabric colors and patterns so you like the arrangement. Take a photo and see how they look together if you like (remember, the garland will naturally flip from back to front, so you'll have some different combinations appearing).

4. When you're happy with the arrangement, stack the circles, working from left to right. Bring them over to your sewing machine and begin stitching them, down the center of each circle, in a continuous row, feeding the next one under the presser foot as the previous one is stitched, so they are touching. (I used a light blue thread that coordinated nicely with all my colors.)

5. Cut the rickrack into two 3-in/7.5-cm pieces and form one into a loop for hanging the garland. Pin the loop to one end of your circle garland and hand-sew the raw edges down with needle and thread. Repeat on the other end with the second piece of rickrack.

6. On one end, cover the raw edges of the loop on each side with a button, and stitch through to sew the two buttons securely in place. Repeat on other end with the remaining two buttons.

7. Hang your garland!

HOLIDAY ORNAMENTS

This little set of red and white mushrooms is easy to stitch up from scraps, and a pair of patchwork stockings gives you the chance to mix and match four favorite prints four different ways. Use some of the same fabrics from your Holiday Garland (page 105) or the Mason Jar & Wine Bottle Cozies (page 115) for an especially pretty holiday set. Hang the ornaments in a window or on a Christmas tree, or add to a special package as a gift topper.

DIMENSIONS:

Mushrooms: 3 in/7.5 cm tall
Stockings: 5 in/12 cm tall

TECHNIQUES USED:

Pattern tracing (page 14)
Inner loop (see steps 2–4)
Seams (page 16)
Turning right-side out (page 17)
Stack and whack patchwork (for the stocking) (page 25)

PATTERN NEEDED:

Mushroom Cap, Mushroom Stem, and Stocking patterns (page 140)

Materials:

Two 4-by-5-in/10-by-12-cm scraps of red fabric, for two mushrooms

Two 4-by-3-in/10-by-7.5-cm scraps of white fabric, for two mushrooms

¼ yd/0.25 m of fusible batting

16 in/40 cm of rickrack (cut into four equal pieces 4 in/10 cm long), for loops

Coordinating thread

One 7-by-5-in/17-by-12-cm piece each of four complementary fabrics of your choice (I used two light blue and two red), for two stockings

Tools:

Pattern paper and pencil

Paper scissors

Fabric scissors

Fabric marker

Iron

Pins

Sewing machine

Hot glue gun or needle and invisible thread

Rotary cutter, cutting mat, and quilt ruler

Continued →

FOR THE MUSHROOM ORNAMENT (MAKES TWO):

1. Trace the Mushroom Cap and Mushroom Stem pattern shapes with pattern paper and pencil, and cut them out with paper scissors.

2. Using your patterns and fabric scissors, cut out two mushroom caps from the red fabric and two mushroom stems from the white fabric, using a fabric marker or pin to transfer the mark for placing your rickrack loop. Then cut out two caps and two stems from the fusible batting. Fuse the batting to the wrong side of each cap and stem piece with an iron, following the manufacturer's instructions.

3. Pin the red cap pieces, right sides together, and tuck a 4-in/10-cm loop of rickrack inside at the marked spot (see fig. 1), so that the raw edges extend slightly above the top edge of the fabrics. Be careful not to twist the rickrack loop.

4. Stitch around the cap with a ¼-in/6-mm seam allowance, leaving the opening unsewn (as marked on the pattern), and backstitching at the beginning and end of the seam to secure. Gently turn right-side out, pushing out the corners with your pencil or a chopstick. The loop will be at the top of the cap.

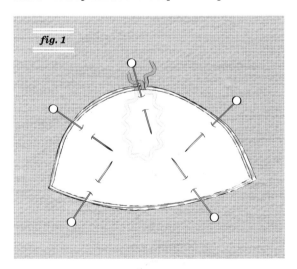

fig. 1

5. Pin the white stem pieces, right sides together, and stitch together with a ¼-in/6-mm seam allowance, leaving the top open (as marked on the pattern). Gently turn right-side out.

6. Fold and press the cap opening raw edges under ¼ in/6 mm. Gently tuck the stem in the cap opening, so that the raw edges are all hidden inside. Pin in place.

7. Hot-glue or use needle and invisible thread to hand-stitch the opening closed to finish the ornament.

8. Repeat steps 1–7 with the second set of red and white fabrics to make another mushroom ornament.

FOR THE STOCKING ORNAMENT (MAKES TWO):

9. Trace the Stocking pattern with pattern paper and pencil, twice, and cut them both out. (Use one pattern oriented like the one on the page and the other reversed, for a mirror image.)

10. Align the four 7-by-5-in/17-by-12-cm pieces of fabric into a stack and use your fabric marker to make cutting lines (see fig. 2, page 110). You'll be cutting three horizontal diagonal lines. Using a rotary cutter, cutting mat, and quilt ruler, slice the stack into four sections.

11. Mix your fabrics into four different combinations. (I chose to arrange mine so that the reds and light blues alternated with each other rather than touched, but any combination works.)

12. When you like the combinations, working in order, place each section right sides together, and stitch with a ¼-in/6-mm seam allowance, until all four sections are joined. Repeat, stitching the remaining three combinations the same way. Press the seams to one side.

Continued ➜

13. Cut four 5-by-5½-in/12-by-14-cm pieces of fusible batting and fuse one to the back of each of the four pieces of stocking patchwork.

14. Choose two of the four patchworks for your first stocking. Pin a stocking pattern over the first patchwork piece, capturing any sections of the print you

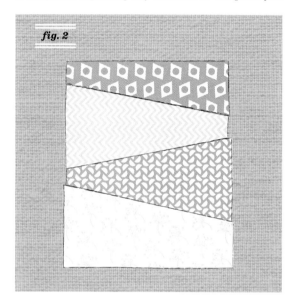

fig. 2

like, and pin the reversed stocking pattern over the second one (see fig. 3). Cut the two stocking shapes out. Make sure to transfer the mark for placing your rickrack loop with a fabric marker or pin.

15. Pin the stocking pieces, right sides together, and tuck a 4-in/10-cm loop of rickrack inside at the point marked on the pattern, as shown in fig. 1.

16. Stitch around the perimeter of the stocking with a ¼-in/6-mm seam allowance, leaving the 1¾-in/4.5 cm marked opening unsewn, backstitching at the beginning and end of the seam to secure. Clip the corners.

17. Gently turn the stocking right-side out, pushing out the corners with your pencil or a chopstick. Fold and press the opening raw edges under ¼ in/6 mm.

18. Hot-glue or hand-stitch the opening closed to finish the ornament.

19. Repeat steps 14–18 to make the second stocking ornament.

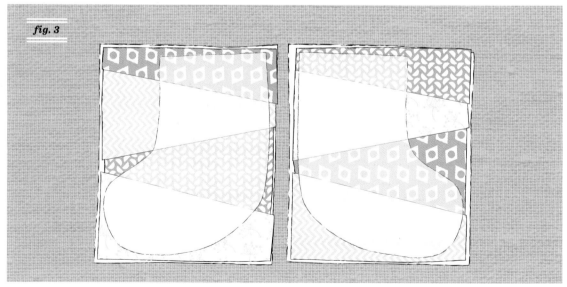

fig. 3

NEW YEAR'S CALENDAR

This simple project "frames" a new or vintage tea towel–style calendar with a favorite fabric and backs it neatly so you can hang or tack it up as you like. Stitch on buttons or other embellishments to mark special dates, birthdays, or anniversaries, and if it's a gift, consider finishing it with little details that remind you of the recipient. Amy Peppler Adams designed this beautiful calendar. You can find one just like it, as well as her other wonderful calendars and fabrics, in her Penny Candy shop on Spoonflower!

DIMENSIONS: variable

TECHNIQUES USED:
Cutting without a pattern (page 14)
Seams (page 16)
Topstitching (page 16)
Turning right-side out (page 17)
Binding (page 20)
Edge-stitching (page 17)
Sewing on a button (page 20)

NOTE:

At the end of the year, you could give this calendar to friends who got married or had a baby, marking the special day with a button or other embellishment. Most vintage fabric calendars were meant to be used as tea towels after the year was over, but saving this one for someone whose year was special is a thoughtful surprise.

I love to make a fabric calendar for each new year, but I've also made special calendars for each of my kids using their birth years. You can find striking vintage fabric calendars at estate sales, thrift stores, Etsy, or eBay.

VINTAGE CALENDAR YEARS TO REUSE:

2013: 1957, 1963, 1974, 1985, 1991, 2002
2014: 1958, 1969, 1975, 1986, 1997, 2003
2015: 1959, 1970, 1981, 1987, 1998, 2009
2016: 1960, 1988
2017: 1950, 1961, 1967, 1978, 1989, 1995, 2006
2018: 1951, 1962, 1973, 1979, 1990, 2001, 2007
2019: 1957, 1963, 1974, 1985, 1991, 2002
2020: 1964, 1992

Continued →

Materials:

One vintage or new calendar printed on fabric

1 yd/1 m quilting cotton (44 in/112 cm wide), for framing and backing

Coordinating thread

One ⁵/₁₆-in/8-mm round dowel, cut to correct length (see step 11)

1 yd/1 m twine, ribbon, or yarn

Buttons or other embellishments

Tools:

Rotary cutter, cutting mat, and quilt ruler

Seam ripper

Iron

Pins

Sewing machine

Scissors

Chopstick

Tape measure

1-in/2.5-cm binding tape maker

Small hand saw (optional)

Hand-sewing needle

1. Trim the edges of your calendar fabric down to about ¾ in/2 cm around the printed design with the rotary cutter, cutting mat, and quilt ruler. If it's a hemmed vintage one, use your seam ripper to unpick the hem stitching. Press with the iron. (Mine measured 21 by 18½ in/53 by 47 cm when trimmed, but sizes may vary.)

2. Cut three to four 2-in-/5-cm-wide strips from your framing fabric, trimming away the selvages (three strips should be plenty, depending on the dimensions of your calendar). Set the rest of the fabric aside.

3. Pin a strip of framing fabric to the top edge of the calendar, right sides together, and stitch using a ¼-in/6-mm seam allowance. Repeat along the bottom edge of the calendar. Press both seams away from the center.

4. Pin and stitch strips of fabric to the left and right sides of the calendar the same way, also pressing the seams away from the center.

5. Topstitch (on the framing fabric) all around the edge of the calendar center, catching the pressed seams on the wrong side of your fabric. Press the calendar.

6. Place the framed calendar on the remaining backing fabric, right sides together, and smooth them flat. Pin in place and use the framed calendar piece as a pattern to cut out a piece of the same size for the backing.

7. Pin the framed calendar and backing pieces, right sides together, around perimeter. Leave a 6-in/15-cm opening in the center of the bottom edge for turning.

8. Stitch around the perimeter of the framed calendar, with a ¼-in/6-mm seam allowance, leaving the opening unsewn, and backstitching at the beginning and end of the seam to secure. Clip the corners and carefully turn the calendar right-side out, pushing out the corners with a chopstick. Fold, press, and pin the opening raw edges under ¼ in/6 mm. Edge-stitch around the entire perimeter.

9. Measure across the top edge of the calendar with a tape measure and make a note of the width (mine was 21 in/53 cm). Cut a strip that length plus ½ in/12 mm from the 2-in-/5-cm-wide fabric (strips left over from steps 3 and 4). Use your binding tape maker to make

Continued ➔

Finished framed calendar width: _____
+ ½ in/12 mm

= **LENGTH TO CUT BINDING TAPE FOR CHANNEL** _____

Finished framed calendar width: _____
+ 1½ in/4 cm

= **LENGTH TO CUT DOWEL** _____

11. Add 1½ in/4 cm to your finished framed calendar width to get your dowel measurement (mine was 22½ in/57 cm). Have a $^5/_{16}$-in/10-mm dowel cut to this length (or use a hand saw to do it yourself) and slip it into the channel, centering the calendar.

12. Tie a length of twine, ribbon, or yarn on the dowel's exposed edges as a hanger (see fig. 1).

13. Hand-stitch buttons or other embellishments on to your calendar with needle and thread to mark family birthdays or other special occasions.

the strip into 1-in-/2.5-cm-wide flat tape, but do not fold it in half a second time.

10. Press each short raw edge of the binding tape under ¼ in/6 mm and pin it in place along the top edge of the calendar back to form a channel for the dowel. Edge-stitch the top and bottom edges of binding tape, backstitching at the beginning and end of the seam to secure. Leave the short ends open.

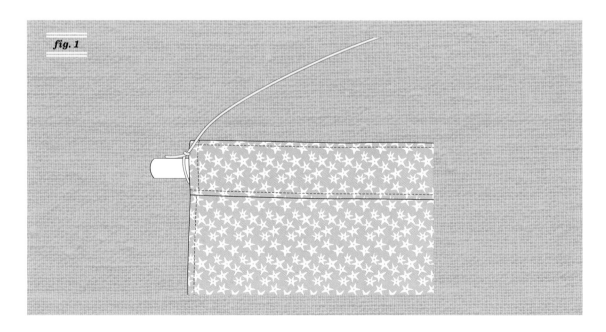

fig. 1

MASON JAR & WINE BOTTLE COZIES

I love to bring wine to a holiday party, or give jars of home-made jam or hot chocolate mix as presents, and I wanted to make something simple and cute to "wrap" those fragile bottles and jars. I came up with this little set of soft-sided cozies with paint-can handles (for the jars) or a ribbon drawstring (for the wine bottles). You can use bits and pieces of favorite leftover fabrics for these cozies—they're a perfect scrap project!

DIMENSIONS:

Half-pint cozy:
4 in/10 cm tall
Pint cozy: 5 in/12 cm tall
Wine bottle cozy:
7 in/17 cm tall

TECHNIQUES USED:

Pattern tracing (page 14)
Cutting without a pattern
(page 14)
Rule of thirds patchwork
(see Note, page 50)
Seams (page 16)
Topstitching (page 16)
Inserting a lining (page 19)
Edge-stitching (page 17)
Binding (page 20)

PATTERNS NEEDED:

Half-Pint Cozy Bottom and
Pint Cozy/Wine Bottle Cozy
Bottom patterns (page 138)

Continued →

PLUM chutney

NOTE:

These cozies are designed for a regular-mouth half-pint jar, a wide-mouth pint jar, and a standard 750-mL bottle of wine.

Materials (for all three cozies):

⅓ yd/0.35 m each of two coordinating print fabrics (44 in/112 cm wide), fabric A and fabric B, for exterior

⅓ yd/0.35 m solid fabric (fabric C) (44 in/112 cm wide), for lining

Coordinating thread

⅓ yd/0.35 m fusible batting

2 small buttons for each jar cozy (optional)

25 in/64 cm ribbon (⅜ in/1 cm wide) for wine cozy

Tools:

Pattern paper and pencil

Paper scissors

Fabric scissors

Rotary cutter, cutting mat, and quilt ruler

Sewing machine

Iron

Pins

1-in/2.5-cm binding tape maker

Hand-sewing needle (optional)

Large safety pin (for wine cozy only)

1. Trace the cozy bottom circle patterns with pattern paper and pencil, and cut them out with paper scissors. Using the circle patterns and fabric scissors, and rotary cutter, cutting mat and quilt ruler, cut the fabrics for each of the three cozies.

HALF-PINT JAR COZY:

Fabric A: one 1¾-by-10½-in/4.5-by-26.5-cm rectangle for upper exterior

Fabric B: one circle for bottom and one 3-by-10½-in/7.5-by-26.5-cm rectangle for lower exterior

PINT JAR COZY:

Fabric A: one circle for bottom and one 4-by-12-in/10-by-30.5-cm rectangle for lower exterior

Fabric B: one 1¾-by-12-in/4.5-by-30.5-cm rectangle for upper exterior

WINE BOTTLE COZY:

Fabric A: one circle for bottom and one 5½-by-12-in/14-by-30.5-cm rectangle for lower exterior

Fabric B: one 1¾-by-12-in/4.5-by-30.5-cm rectangle for upper exterior

ALL COZIES:

You'll need 2-in-/5-cm-wide strips of fabrics A and B for making binding tape, a total of approximately 52 in/132 cm for all three cozies. See step 9 for specifics.

Continued ➜

2. All three of the cozies start the same way: With right sides together, stitch the upper exterior to the lower exterior rectangles using a ¼-in/6-mm seam allowance. Press the seam toward the darker fabric with the iron.

3. Cut one each of lining fabric (fabric C) and fusible batting for the cozy size you're making: Place the joined exterior section over the lining and batting, and cut one of each layer to the same size. Set the lining piece aside. Following manufacturer's instructions, fuse the batting to the wrong side of each exterior cozy panel, and then topstitch along the seam of the joined exterior.

4. Now use your paper cozy bottom template to cut a circle from both batting and lining. Set lining circle aside for now. Following manufacturer's instructions, fuse the batting to the wrong side of the exterior bottom circle.

5. With right sides together, stitch up the short sides of each exterior cozy using a ¼-in/6-mm seam allowance, to form a cylinder (see fig. 1). With right sides together, pin the exterior bottom circle to the bottom of the cozy cylinder, matching the fabrics evenly. Stitch around the perimeter of the circle, using an approximately ¼-in/6-mm seam allowance. Turn the exterior cozy right-side out, smoothing the edges of the bottom circle out.

6. Repeat step 5 with the lining pieces you cut. Do not turn the lining right-side out.

7. Tuck the lining into the exterior cozy and pin it in place around the top perimeter, matching the side seams. Edge-stitch the top perimeter and trim any excess so the top edges are even and smooth.

8. Repeat steps 2–7 for the other two cozies.

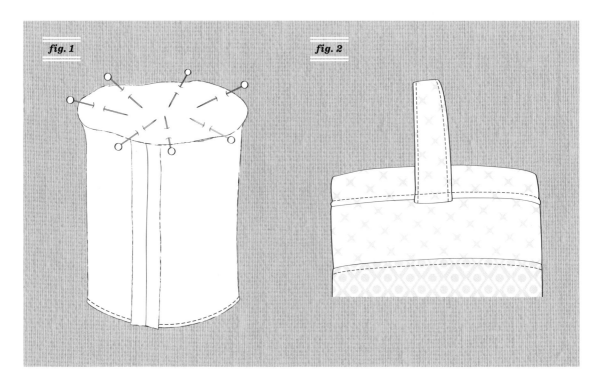

fig. 1

fig. 2

9. Now you'll add binding tape for the handles and edging for the jar cozies, and the drawstring top for the wine bottle version. Using the binding tape maker, make double-folded binding tape with the strips you cut earlier. Measure around the top perimeter of each cozy and note that number. (My half-pint cozy measured 10 in/25 cm, and my pint and wine bottle cozy both measured 11½ in/29 cm. But small differences in sewing matter, so measure yours to be sure.) Cut your binding tape to this measurement plus ½ in/12 mm, and join the short edges to form a ring with a ¼-in/ 6-mm seam allowance.

10. To make the jar cozy handles: For the half-pint jar cut a 7-in/17-cm strip of binding tape; for the pint jar cut an 8-in/20-cm strip of binding tape. Press and edge-stitch the handles along both long sides, closing up the opening along one of the long sides. (The wine cozy does not have a handle.)

11. To finish the jar cozies, place the ring of binding tape over the top edge (sandwiching the cozy layers between the binding tape) and pin in place. Using the cozy side seam as a twelve o'clock position and the front of the cozy as a six o'clock position, mark the three and nine o'clock places with pins. Tuck the raw edges of the handle inside the binding at those two spots, fold each side of the handle up toward the top edge (like a paint-can handle), and pin in place. Stitch around the entire top perimeter of the binding, catching the folded handles as you sew (see fig. 2). Smooth the handles upward at the join and hand-sew a small button over each handle join with needle and thread, if you like.

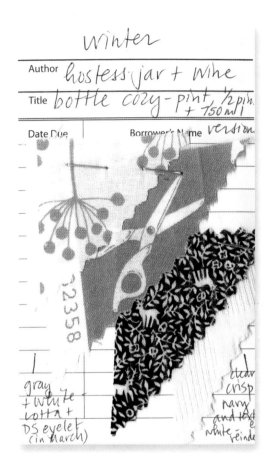

12. To finish the wine cozy with a drawstring, place the binding over the top edge (sandwiching the cozy between the binding tape) and pin in place, leaving open a ¾-in/2-cm section at the front of the cozy (directly opposite the back seam). Stitch the binding tape down, backstitching at the beginning and end of the seam to secure. Use a safety pin to guide the ribbon through the binding channel and back out the opening, put a bottle of wine inside, and tie the ribbon in a bow to close.

CUTE-AS-A-BUTTON HANDBAG

I first designed this Cute-as-a-Button Handbag in 2002, when I had a little craft business and website called Susanstars. I sold these bags at craft fairs and stores in Portland, and I loved their kind-of-vintage, kind-of-modern simplicity. And of course choosing a special button for the triangular flap on each one was my favorite part! Ten years later, I decided to share the pattern in this book, simplified a bit with a snap instead of a buttonhole closure. This is the perfect bag for a holiday party.

DIMENSIONS:
7 1/2 in/19 cm tall

TECHNIQUES USED:
Pattern tracing (page 14)
Seams (page 16)
Box corners (page 18)
Inserting a lining (page 19)
Topstitching (page 16)
Sewing on a snap
(page 20)
Sewing on a button
(page 20)

PATTERN NEEDED:
Cute-as-a-Button Handbag
and Triangle Flap patterns
(page 141)

NOTE:

My friend Megan made this bag using fusible batting instead of interfacing and loved the results. Like the canisters, a project made with batting instead of heavyweight interfacing will still be sturdy but won't be as crisp and defined. If you'd like to try this variation, simply substitute batting for interfacing throughout.

Continued →

Materials:

½ yd/0.5 m home dec fabric (54 to 60 in/ 137 to 152 cm wide), for exterior

½ yd/0.5 m quilting cotton fabric (44 in/112 cm wide), for lining

½ yd/0.5 m heavyweight fusible interfacing (or fusible batting; see Note)

Coordinating thread

1 sew-through or flat shank-style decorative button

1 large sew-in snap (I used a U.S. size 10)

Tools:

Pattern paper and pencil

Paper scissors

Fabric scissors

Rotary cutter, cutting mat, and quilt ruler

Iron

Pins

Sewing machine

Fabric marker (optional)

Hand-sewing needle

Seam ripper

1. Enlarge the handbag and triangle flap patterns using a copier and trace them with pattern paper and pencil. Cut out patterns with paper scissors. With fabric scissors, cut out one of each pattern piece of exterior fabric, lining fabric, and interfacing. Also cut a 3-by-22-in/7.5-by-56-cm strip of both exterior and interfacing fabrics for the bag strap, using a rotary cutter, cutting mat, and quilt ruler.

2. With the iron, fuse the interfacing (following manufacturer's instructions) to the wrong side of the exterior bag, triangle flap, and strap pieces.

3. Fold the exterior bag in half, right sides together, and pin the two long diagonal sides. Stitch the long diagonal sides with a ½-in/12-mm seam allowance, backstitching at the beginning and end of the seam to secure. Press the side seams open. Now create an angular box corner at the bottom of each side of the bag: Align each of the short diagonal sides to each of the straight bottom edges (see fig. 1). Pin the raw edges together and stitch with a ¼-in/6-mm seam allowance, backstitching at the beginning and end. Because the pattern is an angular design, the shape of the box corner will be slightly different from a typical box corner, but it is sewn the same way.

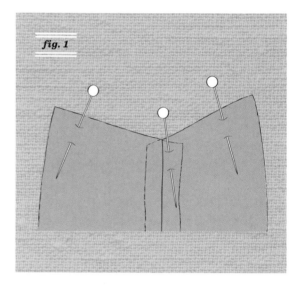

fig. 1

4. Repeat step 3 to make the bag lining.

5. Gently turn the exterior bag right-side out, pushing out the lower corners of the bag with your pencil or a chopstick. Press the bottom edges flat and pin along the bottom edges of the bag at front and back. Topstitch each of the long straight edges of the bottom for definition.

6. Tuck the lining inside the exterior bag, wrong sides together, and match the top raw edges and side seams. Press the top edges under ½ in/12 mm along the exterior bag and the lining pieces, pinning the layers together and catching the raw edges inside the bag. Set aside.

7. Fold and press each long raw edge of the strap under ½ in/12 mm (to the wrong side of fabric). Fold the strap in half lengthwise and pin together along matched folded edges, so raw edges are tucked inside. Topstitch along the pinned edge, pivot at the corner of a short end, and topstitch along the opposite long folded edge of the strap and back to the other end. Set aside.

8. Pin the exterior and lining triangle flaps, right sides together, and stitch around the perimeter of the two longer sides, using a ¼-in/6-mm seam allowance. Trim the triangle flap's tip and gently turn right-side out, pushing out the tip with your pencil or a chopstick, and press flat. Topstitch around the perimeter of the two sides, leaving the opening unsewn.

9. Now unpin the exterior bag and lining at the side seams and tuck ½ in/12 mm of one end of the sewn strap into each side, pinning to secure the strap in place. Then unpin the back left section of the bag, about ½ in/12 mm from the strap, and tuck the triangle flap inside ½ in/12 mm, so the raw edges are hidden between the exterior bag and lining (see fig. 2). Pin triangle flap in place securely.

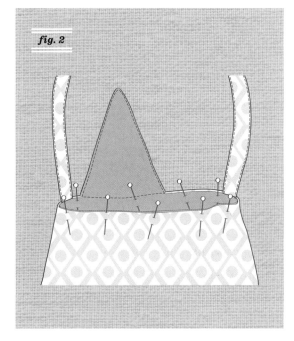

fig. 2

10. With the lining-side up and exterior-side down, topstitch all layers together around the perimeter of the bag opening. Once you've sewn the perimeter, go back and add an extra line of stitching (over the first) for security at both sides where the straps meet the side seams.

11. Pin the triangle flap's bottom tip in place on the front of the bag and use a pin or fabric marker to mark where the snap halves need to line up on the triangle and the front of the bag. With needle and thread, hand-stitch one side of the snap in place on the bag, and knot securely. Then hand-stitch the other side of the snap in place the same way on the triangle flap. Cover the outside of the snap area on the triangle by hand-stitching a beautiful button over the snap stitches.

COZY WOOL SLIPPERS

by Michelle Freedman

My friend Michelle Freedman designed these fabulous slippers using felted Pendleton wool and added a gorgeous three-dimensional rosette on the toe for a special touch. You'll make your own custom-fitted slippers from a pattern you draft yourself. I never dreamed I could make my own slippers, and I love these! They are so cozy for those chilly winter mornings and nights and will keep your toes warm through many winters to come.

DIMENSIONS:
vary, depending on wearer's shoe size

TECHNIQUES USED:
Tracing a pattern (page 14)
Quilting (page 27)
Seams (page 16)
Turning right-side out (page 17)

PATTERN INCLUDED:
Rosette Petals, Lower Leaf, and Upper Leaf patterns (page 139)

Materials:

½ yd/0.5 m medium-weight wool (60 in/152 cm wide) (Michelle used a 12.5-oz/355-g flannel), for slippers

½ yd/0.5 m fusible batting

½ yd/0.5 heavyweight fusible interfacing

Coordinating thread

1 pair of store-bought foam insoles in your size

Puff paint for soles (optional)

Tools:

Flat shoes that fit you well (flip-flops are ideal)

Pattern paper and pencil

Paper scissors

Ruler

Fabric scissors

Pins

Iron

Fabric marker or chalk

Sewing machine

Hand-sewing needle

Continued →

1. Create your slipper pattern pieces: Trace your flip-flop or other flat shoe with pattern paper and pencil. Cut out the shoe shape with paper scissors: This will be your slipper sole pattern (without seam allowance, see fig. 1).

2. Using fig. 1 for reference, measure the length from toe to heel on your sole pattern with a ruler: This is A. Write it down on the measurement table. Divide A in half (this measurement is B) and measure down from the toe to that point. Draw a straight line across the sole there. You'll use this line in step 3.

MEASUREMENT TABLE:

A = measurement from toe to heel
B = half of A; midpoint on the sole pattern
C = width of horizontal line at B
D = C x 2

FILL IN YOUR SIZE:

A = sole measurement from toe to heel _____
A ÷ 2 = **B** _____
C = width of line at halfway point B _____
C x 2 = **D** _____

3. Create your second pattern piece, the slipper top. Measure the line you drew from side to side in step 2, and write down that number (this is C). Multiply C by 2 to get D. To create the pattern for the slipper top, fold a new piece of pattern paper in half and draw a straight line the length of D at the fold edge. Mark the midpoint of that line, and draw a straight line directly up from there, the length of B (as shown in fig. 1, facing page). Draw a generous curved arch upward from one end of your D line back down to the other, intersecting the end of B, as shown. Cut this pattern out (seam allowance is included).

4. Fold the pieces of fusible batting and heavyweight fusible interfacing in half. Using your sole pattern, cut one pair (an original and a mirror image, like your left and right feet) in both interfacing and batting, with fabric scissors, for a total of four pieces.

5. Fold the wool fabric in half, aligning selvage edges. Pin your sole pattern to the folded wool and add a ½-in/12-mm seam allowance all the way around, marking it with your fabric marker or chalk. Cut out two layers of wool with this extra seam allowance. Flip your pattern over and repeat to cut out two more layers of wool for the other sole. Clip a notch on both sides at line C, the halfway point, making the notch the width of the ½-in/12-mm seam allowance.

6. Take one left side and one right side sole of wool, and layer fusible batting over the wrong side of each, centering it over the wool so about ½ in/12 mm shows all the way around. Fuse it in place with an iron, following the manufacturer's instructions. Then, over each of the layered sole pieces, place the interfacing, adhesive-side down, over the batting side of the sole, and fuse it to the sole.

Continued ➜

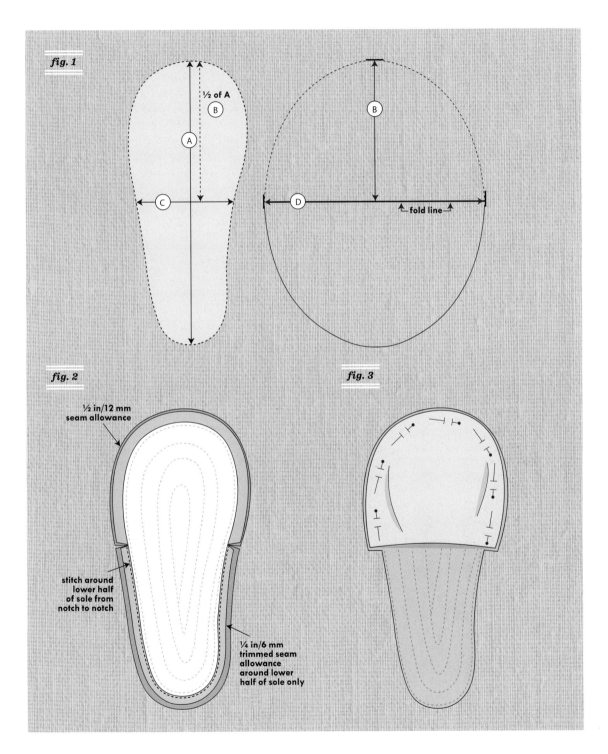

fig. 1

½ of A

Ⓑ

Ⓐ

Ⓒ

Ⓑ

Ⓓ

fold line

fig. 2

½ in/12 mm
seam allowance

stitch around
lower half
of sole from
notch to notch

¼ in/6 mm
trimmed seam
allowance
around lower
half of sole only

fig. 3

7. Set the right sole aside for now and quilt your left layered sole, starting with a line of stitching just inside the perimeter of the interfacing section. Then continue quilting the interior of the sole (in a concentric pattern like the one shown in fig. 2) to securely join all layers, backstitching at the beginning and end of the sewn line. Repeat to quilt the opposite (right) sole the same way. These will be the bottom soles of each slipper.

8. Pin your quilted left sole to the unquilted corresponding left wool sole, right sides together. With the quilted-side up, stitch from the notch you marked in step 5 all the way around the heel to the other notch, using a 1/2-in/12-mm seam allowance (see fig. 2). Trim the top layer of wool seam allowance to 1/4 in/6 mm all the way around the heel, leaving the bottom layer with a 1/2-in/12-mm seam allowance. The toe will be open. Turn the sole right-side out, so your seams are tucked inside the lower half of the sole. Repeat this step for the right sole.

9. Slip your store-bought insole into each slipper sole. You may need to trim the insole down to size to reflect the roundness of the slipper sole.

10. Pin your slipper top pattern to a folded piece of wool. Cut out two identical wool tops (no extra seam allowance necessary).

11. Fold one slipper top in half. With the quilted side of your left sole up, pin the slipper top to it from notch to notch (see fig. 3, page 127). Stitch through all layers, using approximately a 1/2-in/12-mm seam allowance. Backstitch a full 3/4 in/2 cm at the start and end of the curved seam for stability. Repeat this step for the remaining right sole and top pieces.

12. Turn both of your slippers right-side out—you've made a pair of slippers! Now it's time to add a pretty embellishment.

13. Make the rosette embellishment: Trace your rosette circle pattern onto pattern paper, cut it out, and cut out twelve circles in wool (six per slipper). Fold each circle in half, then in half again so they're quartered. With a hand-sewing needle and doubled, knotted thread, sew through all six points and pull the rosette layers together to form the three-dimensional rosette (see fig. 4). Flatten the sixth quartered circle to serve as a base for the rosette. Create your second rosette the same way and set them both aside.

14. Trace the two leaf patterns onto pattern paper, cut them out, and cut out four of each size leaf in wool. Layer one smaller leaf over a larger one and stitch down the center to join them. Repeat to form three more leaf sets.

15. Arrange the rosette with two leaves tucked underneath on a slipper top and pin in place. Hand-stitch all around the base circle, through all layers, being sure to catch the leaves in the stitching. Repeat with the second slipper.

16. If desired, for extra traction, add lines or tiny dots of puff paint on the bottoms of both soles. Let the puff paint dry completely before wearing.

fig. 4

GLOSSARY

APPLIQUÉ An embellishment or fabric layer added to a fabric surface using machine-sewing, hand-sewing, or another method.

BACKSTITCH A very useful sewing stitch that creates a durable join. The sewn row shows as a continuous set of stitches on the right side of the fabric, and shows the reinforced "back" stitches on the wrong side.

BATTING The soft "filling" layer that goes between the front and back fabrics or patchwork sections of a quilt sandwich, adding thickness and warmth to a finished quilt or durability and texture to a smaller craft project. It also comes in fusible varieties, which are perfect for smaller projects.

BIAS OR BINDING TAPE A long double-folded strip of fabric usually used for finishing, edging, or binding a project. The raw edges of a piece of fabric, or several layers, can be tucked inside and then sewed securely in place.

BOX-STITCH A stitched, four-sided box shape with an X inside for added stability, used for adding an element like a handle or waistband.

CRAFT GLUE A good general glue for most materials, which is usually nontoxic. It's best for stationary items that won't bear weight or get wet.

EDGE-STITCH Similar to top-stitching, but stitching very close to the edge of a project or fabric.

EMBROIDERY FLOSS Brightly colored thread for embroidering or other decorative stitching. It usually comes in a six-strand configuration.

FABRIC GLUE A durable glue specially designed for joining layers of fabric together, or adding an embellishment to clothing or other fabric items. It's often machine-washable or dry-cleanable—check the label.

FABRIC SCISSORS Sharp scissors for cutting fabric smoothly. To keep them in sharp condition, do not use them for paper or other cutting.

FELT A thick, opaque fabric made of acrylic, wool, or a blend of materials that does not fray, perfect to use for sewing or other crafts.

FOUNDATION PIECING
Stitching a patchwork pattern (like string quilting) to a backing piece of muslin for added stability.

FUSIBLE INTERFACING
A fusible layer that adds stiffness and body to a fabric project.

HOME DEC FABRIC
Heavier-weight fabrics such as denim, canvas, or corduroy that are often wider than quilting cotton (about 54 to 60 in/137 to 152 cm), useful for making bags or home décor projects.

HOT GLUE Special glue sticks for a hot glue gun, which melt when heated, and are ideal for adding decorative elements or sealing openings on craft sewing projects.

PATTERN PAPER A special paper that is ideal for tracing or creating your own reusable patterns. Most useful when it's marked with measurements for correct sizing.

PIECING Joining pieces of fabric together with narrow (usually ¼-in/6-mm) seams to create a quilt block or quilt top.

PINKING SHEARS Scissors with special jagged blades that cut fabric with a neat and decorative zigzag edge that is unlikely to fray.

QUILT BLOCK A patchwork design (usually a square or rectangle, trimmed to size after piecing) to use as part of a quilt or as a home décor project.

QUILT SANDWICH Three layers joined for quilting: usually a patchwork top, batting in the middle, and a backing fabric (pieced or whole-cloth).

QUILTING Stitching through all layers of a quilt sandwich to join them securely, in the pattern or style of your choice.

ROTARY CUTTER A small, precise hand tool for cutting fabric, especially along an edge or pattern line, with a very sharp, rotating blade. Use on a self-healing cutting mat or other durable surface, never a bare floor or tabletop.

RUNNING STITCH A simple forward stitch for hand-basting two layers of fabric together, often begun and ended with backstitching to secure the sewn line.

SEAM ALLOWANCE The consistent distance from the edge of the fabric to the seam line, often ¼ in/6 mm for patchwork, ½ in/ 12 mm for craft projects, and ⅝ in/16 mm for garment sewing.

SELVAGE The finished woven edges on either side of fabric off the bolt, often woven more tightly than the rest of the material, and sometimes printed with information about the designer or manufacturer.

STRING BLOCKS
Patchwork blocks made using string-piecing techniques to join strips or "strings" of fabric in a diagonal pattern.

TOPSTITCHING A basic machine-sewing technique that adds stability to seams, joins fabric layers, or simply adds a polished look by adding a stitched row parallel to a seam.

TURN (RIGHT-SIDE OUT)
The process of turning a sewn project from wrong-side out to right-side out with raw edges hidden inside, often using a chopstick or pencil to open corners.

ZIGZAG STITCH A sewing machine stitch ideal for joining layers of fabric, or for appliquéing or edging a design, especially with a narrow, tight stitch setting.

WHOLE CLOTH A single-fabric version of a project, rather than patchwork or pieced.

RESOURCES

Here are my favorite books, websites, shops, and other resources for sewing and patchwork:

BOOKS

1, 2, 3 Sew, by Ellen Luckett Baker
A wonderful guide to basic sewing, with each project teaching a new skill or idea.

The Art of Manipulating Fabric, by Colette Wolff
Fantastic techniques for working with fabric to create all kinds of lovely effects.

Bend the Rules Sewing, by Amy Karol
Amy's take on sewing is fresh and fun, and the tips and ideas she shares are fantastic, too.

Button It Up, by Susan Beal
My favorite button craft projects, with plenty of sewing and embellishment ideas mixed in.

The Colette Sewing Handbook, by Sarai Mitnick
A perfect resource for garment sewing as well as valuable information on choosing fabrics and learning techniques.

Denyse Schmidt Quilts and *Modern Quilts, Traditional Inspiration,* by Denyse Schmidt
A beautiful pair of books offering stunning quilt designs from a modern quilting icon and designer extraordinaire.

Lotta Sews, by Lotta Jansdotter
Inspiring projects in Lotta's signature style.

Mastering the Art of Fabric Printing and Design, by Laurie Wisbrun
A fascinating guide to creating your own original fabric designs.

Modern Log Cabin Quilting, by Susan Beal
My quilts and patchwork projects using one of my favorite block patterns, the log cabin—simple, endlessly versatile, and beautiful.

Modern Minimal, by Alissa Haight Carlton
An inspiring take on using simple, stunning solids and angular shapes in quilts and patchwork.

The Modern Quilt Workshop,
Quilts Made Modern, and *Transparency Quilts,*
by Weeks Ringle and Bill Kerr
This trio of quilting books is remarkable. They offer solid techniques, intriguing color theory, and fantastic quilt patterns.

Pantone: The Twentieth Century in Color,
by Leatrice Eiseman and Keith Recker
A color-driven history, relating the story and ideas of our culture in the most visual context.

The Practical Guide to Patchwork and
Modern Patchwork, by Elizabeth Hartman
Two wonderful books for the modern quilter. Elizabeth's attention to detail and eye for design are fantastic.

Sewing in a Straight Line, by Brett Bara
An amazing array of sophisticated projects, all using straight-seams-only sewing.

Sewing Made Simple, by Tessa Evelegh
A generous resource of sewing techniques and ideas.

So Pretty! Felt, by Amy Palanjian
A charming collection of projects to make with felt, including contributing designers from all over the world.

Stitched in Time and *Embroidery Companion,*
by Alicia Paulson
Alicia shares her beautiful aesthetic in these two collections of heirloom-quality needlework and sewing projects.

Vera: A Signature Life, by Susan Seid
An inspiring biography and portfolio of work from an outstanding designer and textile artist.

Vintage Craft Workshop, by Cathy Callahan
Cathy updates the best craft projects of the 1960s and '70s into modern versions—super inspiring.

SHOPS

My stellar local fabric stores are Cool Cottons (*coolcottons.biz*) and Bolt (*boltfabricboutique.com*). If you are ever in Portland, Oregon, I highly recommend visiting these stores in person!

Etsy (*Etsy.com)* has vintage calendar tea towels, vintage sheets like the one I used to back my Picnic Quilt (page 77), and an endless supply of amazing sewing notions and fabric (both new and vintage). *eBay.com,* thrift stores, and estate sales are other go-tos for unusual finds!

Nancy Stovall does beautiful long-arm quilting in her Portland, Oregon, studio, and is happy to work with quilters near and far.
Justquiltingpdx.com

Nifty Thrifty Dry Goods offers lovely vintage buttons and new buttons, twill tape, lace, trims, and other notions.
Niftythriftydrygoods.com

Pink Chalk Fabrics also has a fantastic selection of prints and solids (including Cotton Couture).
Pinkchalkfabrics.com

Nearly all the solid fabrics in this book's designs are Michael Miller Cotton Couture, which is fabulous to sew with.
Michaelmillerfabrics.com

Purl Soho is a gorgeous boutique fabric and yarn shop in New York well worth a visit in person, but you can shop for their perfectly curated craft supplies of all types online, or follow their wonderful project blog, the Purl Bee.
purlsoho.com

Pendleton sells their amazing wool fabric at their Woolen Mill Store in Portland, Oregon, but you can find selected wool fabrics online. You can also check out their inspiring blog with lots of fabric swatches, projects, and ideas at *thewoolenmillstore .blogspot.com.*
Pendleton-usa.com

Spoonflower has fabulous fabric for sale by independent designers: Search for a motif or style you like. And it's a great place to buy tea towel calendars, too! You can find one just like the one used in the New Year's Calendar project (see page 111).
Spoonflower.com

GENERAL INSPIRATION

Coats and Clark has a fabulous blog, Sewing Secrets, on their company website.
Coatsandclark.com

Modern Quilt Guilds: Find a modern quilt guild chapter near you (or start your own!). I love our chapter, Portland Modern Quilt Guild (*portlandmodernquiltguild.blogspot.com*), and I've found endless inspiration from our meetings, quilt show-and-tells, and sewing days.
Themodernquiltguild.com

Sew Daily is the online partner to stylish *Stitch* magazine, one of my favorite sewing publications. They host lots of craft videos and project extras.
Sewdaily.com

Sew, Mama, Sew! is a wonderful sewing and quilting blog with free patterns and tutorials.
Sewmamasew.com

Threadbias is a lovely, friendly sewing community where you can share photos, fabric swatches, and project details as well as meet other sewists nearby.
Threadbias.com

True Up is a fantastic resource for all things fabric.
Trueup.net

Learn new sewing or quilting techniques online! Craftsy (*craftsy.com*) and Creativebug (*creativebug .com*) both offer wonderful video classes and workshops, from beginner to advanced skill levels.

ACKNOWLEDGMENTS

This book came together over a very eventful year, and I am so grateful to my friends, family, and craft allies for their wonderful support!

First, thank you to everyone who made *Sewing for All Seasons* possible. Thank you to my wonderful editor at Chronicle, Laura Lee Mattingly, for her insights, ideas, and inspiration. Thank you to my art director, Jennifer Tolo Pierce, for collaborating on the colorful and seasonal aesthetic that truly defined the projects. Alexis Hartman's precise and lovely illustrations brought the written instructions to life, Dolin O'Shea's careful tech edits and Ellen Wheat's thoughtful copy edits sharpened everything nicely, and Jennifer Causey's beautiful photographs are such a joyful part of the book. And, thank you as always to my agent, Stacey Glick, who is a true advocate. I am so grateful to all of you!

Thank you to my friends and creative collaborators: Michelle Freedman of Design Camp PDX designed and sewed two stunning original projects, the Sewing Organizer and the Cozy Wool Slippers, for the book's collection. They are wonderful and so very Michelle! Thank you to my friends who helped me create and refine my original inspiration boards for spring, summer, fall, and winter: Maggie Santolla, Meredith MacDonald, Mary Ramsay, Diane Gilleland, and Fiona Gillespie.

Another thank-you to my fabulous pattern testers, Pétra Anderson, Heather Davidson, Jennifer Carlton-Bailly, Megan Dye, Brittany Scott, Rachel Kerley, Jill Collins, and Michelle Freedman, for making your own fantastic versions of my projects and giving me such valuable feedback along the way. Thank you to Alexandra Kloch for letting me use her AccuQuilt fabric cutter to zip out all those super-precise circles for my garland—a revelation!

I'm also so grateful to Pétra, Heather, Brittany, and Rachel for joining me at a super fun afternoon quilting bee, stitching the last few dozen colorful string blocks for the Picnic Quilt at my dining room table. And I can't thank Nancy Stovall enough for the beautiful quilting on it, too—the perfect pattern for summer.

Speaking of these ladies, I was so lucky to serve as president of our beloved Portland Modern Quilt Guild the year I wrote and sewed everything for this book. I am constantly inspired by our talented members and their beautiful work, and the third Thursday is my favorite day of every month!

Thank you so much to Kathy and Christine at Michael Miller Fabrics for providing some of their wonderful Cotton Couture solid fabric for my larger projects—it's a dream to sew with. Thank you to Julie, Tawnya, and everyone at the Pendleton Woolen Mill Store for their kind and generous support, and beautiful fabrics, as well. Thanks to Monica Solorio-Snow for her gift of Happy Mochi Yum Yum fabrics! Last, a huge thank-you to Amy Pepplar Adams of Pennycandy for sending me her fabulous and original Spoonflower calendar fabric, two years before the dates were right!

I am so fortunate to have my husband, Andrew, as my partner in life and creativity alike. His constant love and support are a huge gift in my life. My daughter Pearl's sunny charm and intense love of pretty colors fueled my project ideas. (She was born in the right season for sure.) And to my sweet little boy, Everett, who grew from a cuddly baby to an independent and curious two-year-old as this collection of projects came together: This book is for you.

PATTERNS

**VINTAGE SCARF
HEADBAND**

enlarge all by 50%

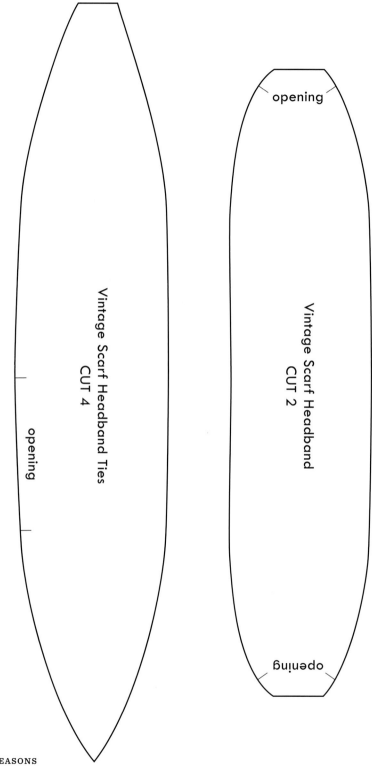

Vintage Scarf Headband Ties
CUT 4

opening

Vintage Scarf Headband
CUT 2

opening

opening

SUNGLASSES CASE

enlarge by 15%

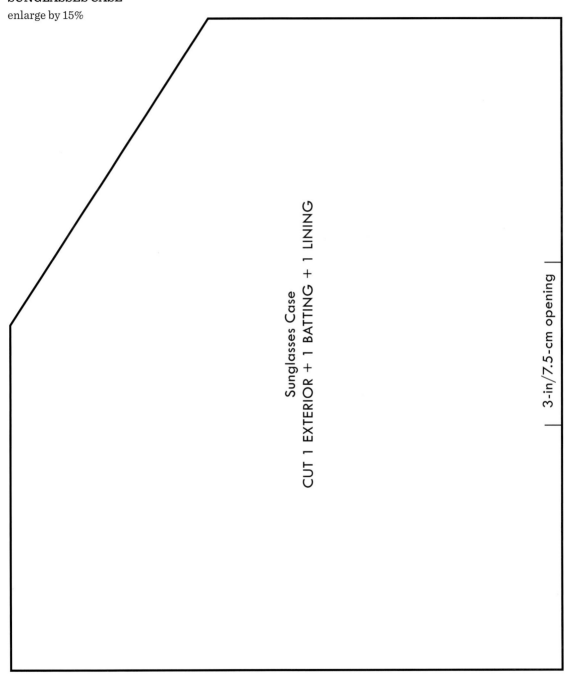

Sunglasses Case
CUT 1 EXTERIOR + 1 BATTING + 1 LINING

3-in/7.5-cm opening

**COFFEE CUP COZY, MASON JAR
& WINE BOTTLE COZIES**

enlarge all by 30%

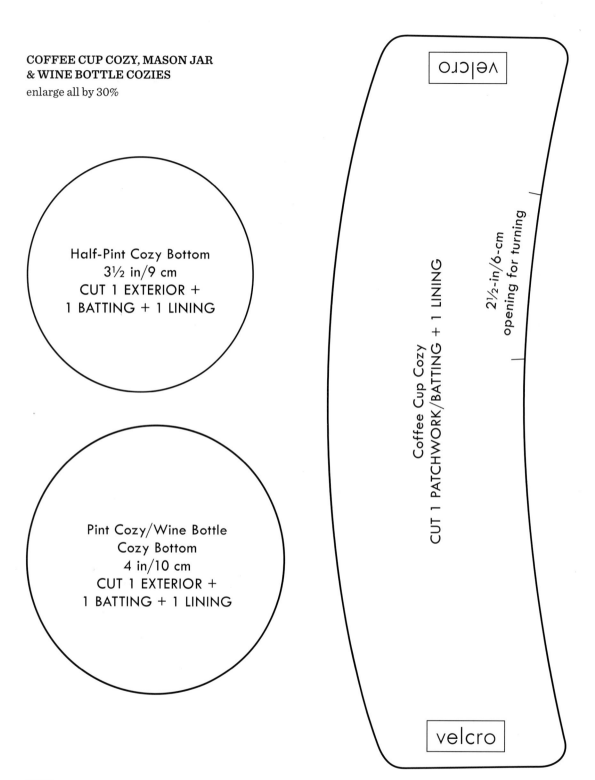

Half-Pint Cozy Bottom
3½ in/9 cm
CUT 1 EXTERIOR +
1 BATTING + 1 LINING

Pint Cozy/Wine Bottle
Cozy Bottom
4 in/10 cm
CUT 1 EXTERIOR +
1 BATTING + 1 LINING

velcro

Coffee Cup Cozy
CUT 1 PATCHWORK/BATTING + 1 LINING

2½-in/6-cm
opening for turning

velcro

HOLIDAY GARLAND

do not enlarge

Holiday Garland
CUT 36 IN
DOUBLE-SIDED
FABRICS

COZY WOOL SLIPPERS

do not enlarge

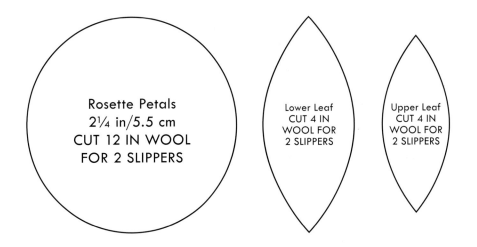

Rosette Petals
2¼ in/5.5 cm
CUT 12 IN WOOL
FOR 2 SLIPPERS

Lower Leaf
CUT 4 IN
WOOL FOR
2 SLIPPERS

Upper Leaf
CUT 4 IN
WOOL FOR
2 SLIPPERS

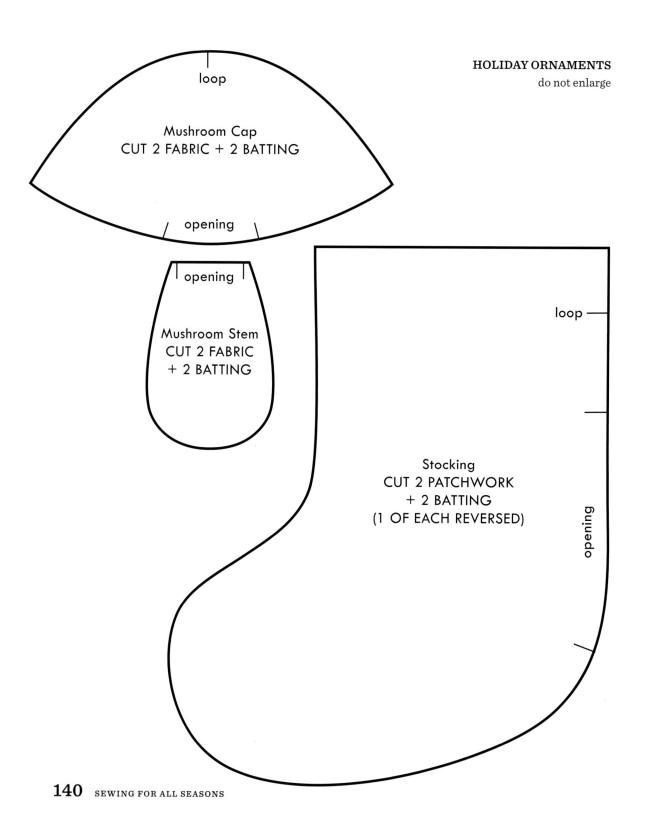

loop

Mushroom Cap
CUT 2 FABRIC + 2 BATTING

opening

opening

Mushroom Stem
CUT 2 FABRIC
+ 2 BATTING

loop

Stocking
CUT 2 PATCHWORK
+ 2 BATTING
(1 OF EACH REVERSED)

opening

CUTE-AS-A-BUTTON HANDBAG

enlarge all by 70%

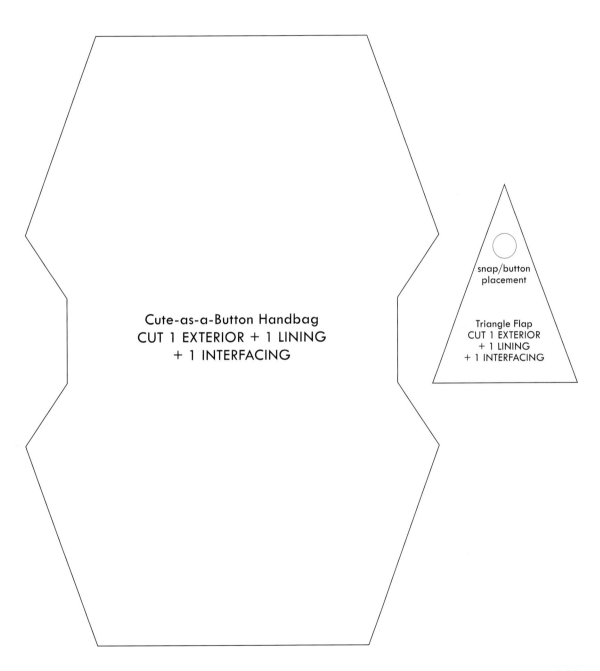

Cute-as-a-Button Handbag
CUT 1 EXTERIOR + 1 LINING
+ 1 INTERFACING

snap/button
placement

Triangle Flap
CUT 1 EXTERIOR
+ 1 LINING
+ 1 INTERFACING

INDEX